D1503168

Dr. Ackerman's Book of
Collies

LOWELL ACKERMAN DVM

BB-109

Overleaf: Two Rough Collies showing off their well-groomed lustrous coats. These are Zigline's Gold La-La and Zigline's Heart of Midnight owned by Monica Lonnstrom.

The author has exerted every effort to ensure that medical information mentioned in this book is in accord with current recommendations and practice at the time of publication. However, in view of the ongoing advances in veterinary medicine, the reader is urged to consult with his veterinarian regarding individual health issues.

Photographers: Dennis Albert, Terry Albert, Tara Darling, Isabelle Francais, and Karen Taylor.

Special thanks to Dr. Henry for taking time to work with Miss Francais on photographs for this publication.

The presentation of pet products in this book is strictly for instructive purposes only; it does not constitute an endorsement by the author, publisher, owners of dogs portrayed, or any other contributors.

t.f.h.

© **1996 by LOWELL ACKERMAN DVM**

Distributed in the UNITED STATES to the Pet Trade by T.F.H. Publications, Inc., One T.F.H. Plaza, Neptune City, NJ 07753; distributed in the UNITED STATES to the Bookstore and Library Trade by National Book Network, Inc. 4720 Boston Way, Lanham MD 20706; in CANADA to the Pet Trade by H & L Pet Supplies Inc., 27 Kingston Crescent, Kitchener, Ontario N2B 2T6; Rolf C. Hagen Inc., 3225 Sartelon St. Laurent-Montreal Quebec H4R 1E8; in CANADA to the Book Trade by Vanwell Publishing Ltd., 1 Northrup Crescent, St. Catharines, Ontario L2M 6P5 ; in ENGLAND by T.F.H. Publications, PO Box 15, Waterlooville PO7 6BQ; in AUSTRALIA AND THE SOUTH PACIFIC by T.F.H. (Australia), Pty. Ltd., Box 149, Brookvale 2100 N.S.W., Australia; in NEW ZEALAND by Brooklands Aquarium Ltd. 5 McGiven Drive, New Plymouth, RD1 New Zealand; in Japan by T.F.H. Publications, Japan—Jiro Tsuda, 10-12-3 Ohjidai, Sakura, Chiba 285, Japan; in SOUTH AFRICA by Lopis (Pty) Ltd., P.O. Box 39127, Booysens, 2016, Johannesburg, South Africa. Published by T.F.H. Publications, Inc.

MANUFACTURED IN THE
UNITED STATES OF AMERICA
BY T.F.H. PUBLICATIONS, INC.

CONTENTS

DEDICATION

To my wonderful wife Susan and my three adorable children, Nadia, Rebecca, and David.

PREFACE

Keeping your Collie healthy is the most important job that you, as owner, can do. Whereas there are many books available that deal with breed qualities, conformation, and show characteristics, this may be the only book available dedicated entirely to the preventative health care of the Collie. This information has been compiled from a variety of sources and assembled here to provide you with the most up-to-date advice available.

This book will take you through the important stages of selecting your pet, screening it for inherited medical and behavioral problems, meeting its nutritional needs, and seeing that it receives optimal medical care.

So, enjoy the book and use the information to keep your Collie the healthiest it can be for a long, full and rich life.

Lowell Ackerman DVM

BIOGRAPHY

Dr. Lowell Ackerman is a world-renowned veterinary clinician, author, lecturer and radio personality. He is a Diplomate of the American College of Veterinary Dermatology and is a consultant in the fields of dermatology, nutrition and genetics. Dr. Ackerman is the author of 34 books and over 150 book chapters and articles. He also hosts a national radio show on pet health care and moderates a site on the World Wide Web dedicated to pet health care issues (http://www.familyinternet.com/pet/pet-vet.htm).

BREED HISTORY

THE GENESIS OF THE MODERN COLLIE

The exact origins of the Collie are lost in history, but it is clearly a descendant of the herding dogs and shepherds that were working hard all  across Medieval Europe. These, in turn, originated from the Roman herding dogs. The best estimate is that the Scottish working dogs known as Collies

Facing page: Today's Collie enjoys a close rapport with the flock he herds: his loved ones. This is Kelby and Lu Anne Novello sharing a picturesque moment.

Because of their heritage with livestock, Collies get along well with many four-legged creatures. This is Colley Girl enjoying an afternoon with Spice, the pony.

probably were selectively bred in the 1700s. The name Collie is likely derived from the word *"collis,"* meaning high ground. Others have theorized that it came from the Latin *Collaboro* (to labor with, as in collaborate) or *Collatio* (to put together, as in collate). The true story of the derivation of the word Collie is lost in antiquity.

Whatever their exact ancestry, it is the sheep-herding dogs of the Scottish Highlands that gave rise to the Collie we know today. The shepherding skills were accentuated with natural selection and selective breeding practices. The original Collies were quite a bit smaller than today's examples, measuring approximately 14 inches at the shoulder and weighing 25–45 pounds. This was true for both smooth-and rough-coated varieties. The Smooth variety of Collie was used to drive livestock to market (a drover dog) while the

Rough Collie was a sheep-herding dog working directly with the flocks. At this point, it is not known whether the Smooth and Rough Collies originated as the same breed or whether they started out as separate breeds. Regardless of the true answer, the Smooths and Roughs were interbred in the early days and produced mixed litters of Smooth and Rough offspring.

Queen Victoria was credited with advancing the popularity of the breed when she fell in love with the Collies at her Scottish retreat. Until then, the Collies were considered pets of farmers, not royalty. The first Collies were introduced to America in the late 1870s, and the first registration of the breed in the American Kennel Club Stud Book occurred in 1885.

The Collie excels as a farm dog and proves adaptable to many tasks. These two handsome males are Nathan and Trevor owned by Kim Hundley.

MIND &
BODY

**PHYSICAL AND BEHAVIORAL TRAITS
OF THE COLLIE**

The Collie is such a family oriented dog that it's no wonder generations have fallen in love with the most popular one of all, Lassie. The breed lives up to its reputation as a protector of hearth and home, as anyone who owns one of these loyal, loving, smart, stylish, and gentle dogs will tell you.

Facing page: The quintessential children's dog, the Collie wins every popularity contest. This reliable escort sees his young charge to the bus stop.

At ten years of age, this is Pascal owned by Louis Gordon. Longevity and good health are excellent ways to judge a good Collie. Pascal survived KCS surgery when six years old and still continued to live a normal, happy life.

CONFORMATION AND PHYSICAL CHARACTERISTICS

This is not a book about show dogs, so information here will not deal with the conformation of champions and how to select one. The purpose of this chapter is to provide basic information about the stature of a Collie and qualities of a physical nature.

Clearly, beauty is in the eye of the beholder, and since standards come and standards go, measuring your dog against some imaginary yardstick does little for you or your dog. Just because your dog isn't a show champion doesn't mean that he or she is any less of a family member. And, just because a dog is a champion doesn't mean that he or she is not a genetic time bomb waiting to go off.

When breeders and those interested in showing Collies are selecting dogs, they are looking for those qualities that match the breed "standard." This standard, however, is of an imaginary Collie and it changes from time to time and from country to country. Thus, the conformation and physical characteristics that pet owners should concentrate on are somewhat different and much more practical.

Collies were originally bred to be medium-sized dogs but, over time, they were bred to become progressively larger. Most adult males are 24–26 inches at the withers and bitches are about two inches smaller. The normal weight range for the breed is 60–75 pounds but a better target is about 65 pounds for females and 70 pounds for males. Larger dogs are not necessarily better dogs. Collies were never intended to be considered "giants" and the increased size might promote some medical problems which tend to be more common in larger dogs. The head shape of Collies is long and elongated and this tendency is referred to by veterinarians as "dolicocephalic."

Collies are intended to be medium-large dogs. Do not be impressed by size alone. If the dog cannot move with grace and agility, it may be symptomatic of other problems. Owner, Bernice Terry.

COAT COLOR, CARE AND CONDITION

There are four "approved" colors of Collie: sable and white, tri-color, blue merle, and white. Sable is dominant over tri-color and the merle factor is a dominant modifier of either the sable or the tri-color. When two sables are bred, the resultant offspring include predominantly sables with some tri-color. When two tri-colors are bred, the result is all tri-color pups.

The genetics of coat color are fairly complex in the Collie and are controlled by three principal genes — the agouti gene (A), the white spotting gene (S), and the merling gene (M). One gene determines if the base color is sable (Ay) or tri-color (at); sable is dominant. Another determines if there is no white present (S) or if there is (si). Finally, another determines whether or not the color is merled (Mm) or non-merled (MM or mm).

Grooming a Collie can be *rough*! Owners must commit to the proper care of such an abundantly coated purebred. This is Zimmy at age 11 after being rescued from a humane society.

Collies are colorful, as this Scotch trio of tri-colors reveals. Whether black and tan, sable or merle, Collies exhibit different shading and color combinations, always with white. Owner, Bernice Terry.

Without becoming geneticists we can still appreciate how the colors occur in the breed with some basic rules. Each pup receives half a set of genes from its mother and half from its father. Sable is the dominant trait, referred to by the capital letter "*Ay.*" A small "*at*" signifies tri-color, but is recessive; it takes two (*at at*) for the dog to be tri-color. Since sable is the dominant color, a dog will be sable with either two (*Ay Ay*) or one (*Ay at*) sable genes. Dogs will only be tri-color if they have both recessive genes (*at at*). One important point here. You can't tell if a dog is Ay Ay or Ay at by looking; they're both sable. This demonstrates the difference between genotype and phenotype. Genotype refers to the genetic combinations which we can't see (e.g., *Ay Ay* , *Ay at* , *at at*) while phenotype refers to the products which we can see (e.g., sable, tri-color). If a mating of two sable Collies produces any tri-color pups, you can infer that both parents had to be carriers (*Ay at*) since a recessive gene must have been inherited from each parent.

What about merles? Well, the genetics are identical. Not only do parents pass either an "*Ay*" or "*at*" to their pups, they do the same with the merle gene "*M*." The undiluted colors (sables and tri-colors) are co-dominant with the merled colors (merled sables and tri-colors, but the merle gene affects black coloration most so it is most obvious in the tri-color). Dogs that carry the genes *mm*

There are also two coat types of Collie: Smooth and Rough. Neither have very stringent grooming requirements. The Rough Collie will benefit from a thorough brushing once a week. This helps remove mats, clean out shed fur and add luster to the coat. The Smooth Collie requires even less attention. Flea comb regularly to search for fleas, but excessive grooming

The merle coloration is genetically linked to many problems, including deafness, blindness and sterility. If you are attracted to this coloration, be extra cautious in making your selection. Owner, Joseph Reno.

have no merling. The merle coloration is only seen in animals that are heterozygotes (*Mm*). It is undesirable to create dogs that have both dominant merle genes (*MM*) because they not only cause an all-white coat, but the animals have a high susceptibility to deafness, eye problems and sterility.

only damages the all-weather coat the Collie was born with.

BEHAVIOR AND PERSONALITY OF THE ACTIVE COLLIE

Behavior and personality are two qualities which are hard to standardize within a breed. Although generalizations are difficult to make, most Collies are alert and people-oriented. They make great working dogs because they do have the capacity to be loyal, determined, watchful and obedient. However, it is their social nature that makes them want to work with people. This is not the breed to be tied in the backyard to serve as a watchdog. Similarly, this is not the breed to be abandoned anywhere regardless of intentions. Collies can dig under a wall or jump a high fence. Whether they are shy or vicious has something to do with their genetics, but also is determined by the socialization and training they receive. In general, Collies are extremely gentle, intelligent and friendly dogs.

Behavior and personality are incredibly important in dogs and there seem to be quite evident extremes in the Collie. Few Collies are ever vicious but they have been bred as working dogs so some may not do well with a lot of spare time on their hands and little purpose to their days. The ideal Collie is neither aggressive nor neurotic but rather a loving family member with good self-esteem and acceptance of position in the family "pack." Because the Collie is a powerful dog and can cause much damage, it is worth spending the time when selecting a pup to pay attention to any evidence of personality problems. It is also imperative that *all* Collies be obedience trained. Like any dog, they have the potential to be unruly without appropriate training; consider obedience classes mandatory for your sake and that of your dog.

Involve your Collies in your every-day and weekend outings. These are intelligent dogs that thrive on activity and chores. An active Collie is a happy Collie. Owner, Kevin Novello.

Although many Collies are happy to sleep the day away in bed or on a sofa, most enjoy having a purpose in their day and that makes them excellent working dogs. They generally need long daily walks and runs and aren't usually happy with idle time. All Collies should attend obedience classes and they need to learn limits to unacceptable behaviors. A well-loved and well-controlled Collie is certain to be a valued family member.

For pet owners, there are several activities to which your Collie is well-suited. They not only make great walking and jogging partners but they also are excellent community volunteers. The loyal and loving Collie will also be your personal guard dog if properly trained; aggressiveness and viciousness do not fit into the equation.

For Collie enthusiasts who want to get into more competitive aspects of the dog world, showing, herding, hunting, obedience, guarding and tracking are all activities that can be considered.

How about a herd of Collies? Consider adding a second Collie to the family (or a third!) to keep your Collie company. Two Collies are always busier than one! Owner, Bernice Terry.

Obedience training is vital for every dog, and with a Collie it's refreshingly simple. These dogs respond naturally to commands and look forward to lessons with much enthusiasm. This is Cullen and his owner-trainer Sally Richardson.

SELECTING

**WHAT YOU NEED TO KNOW TO FIND
THE BEST COLLIE PUPPY**

Owning the perfect Collie rarely happens by accident. On the other hand, owning a genetic dud is almost always the result of an impulse purchase and failure to do even basic research. Buying this book is a major step in understanding the situation and making intelligent choices.

Facing page: Collie puppies can seduce even a browsing non-dog person. The commitment goes beyond this puppy's smile. You owe it to your puppy to be more informed about his health and needs than he is! Owners, Pattie and Jerry Fitzgerald.

Meeting the dam of your future puppy is tantamount to seeing your puppy as an adult. Breeders that perform necessary screening know of any defects in their lines and do not breed affected dogs. Owner, Joseph Reno.

SOURCES

Recently, a large survey was done to determine whether there were more problems seen in animals adopted from pet stores, breeders, private owners or animal shelters. Somewhat surprisingly, there didn't appear to be any major difference in total number of problems seen from these sources. What was different were the kinds of problems seen in each source. Thus, you can't rely on any one source because there are no standards by which judgments can be made. Most veterinarians will recommend that you select a "good breeder," but there is no way to identify such an individual. A breeder of champion show dogs may also be a breeder of genetic defects.

The best approach is to select a pup from a source that regularly performs genetic screening and has documentation to prove it. If you are intending to be a pet owner, don't worry about whether your pup is show quality. A mark here or there that might disqualify the pup as a show winner has absolutely no impact on its ability to be a loving and healthy pet. Also, the vast majority of dogs will be neutered and not used for breeding anyway. Concentrate on the things that are important.

MEDICAL SCREENING

Whether you are dealing with a breeder, a breed rescue group, a shelter or a pet store, your approach should be the same. You want to identify a Collie that you can live with and screen it for medical and behavioral problems before you make it a permanent family member. If the source you select has not done the important testing needed, make sure they will offer you a health/temperament guarantee before you remove the dog from the premises to have the work done yourself. If this is not acceptable, or they are offering an exchange-only policy, keep moving; this isn't the right place for you to get a dog. As soon as you purchase a Collie, pup or adult, go to your veterinarian for thorough evaluation and testing.

A vital, energetic puppy with an alert, friendly temperament makes the best choice for a pet. Owner, Joseph Reno.

Pedigree analysis is best left to true enthusiasts but there are some things that you can do, even as a novice. Inbreeding is to be discouraged so check out your four- or five-generation pedigree and look for names that appear repeatedly. Reputable breeders will usually not allow inbreeding at least three generations back in the puppy's pedigree. Also ask the breeder to provide OFA and CERF registration numbers on all ancestors in the pedigree for which testing is done. If there are a lot of gaps, the breeder has some explaining to do.

The screening procedure is easier if you select an older dog. Animals can be registered for hips and elbows as young as two years of age by the Orthopedic Foundation for Animals and by one year of age by Genetic Disease Control. This is your insurance against hip dysplasia and elbow dysplasia later in life. Although Collies now have a relatively low incidence of these orthopedic problems, it is because of the efforts of conscientious breeders who have been doing the appropriate testing. A verbal testimonial that they've never heard of the condition in their lines is not adequate and probably means they really don't know if they have a problem. Move along.

Regardless of where you purchase a puppy, a visit to the veterinarian is the first priority. Only your veterinarian can tell you for certain that the puppy is parasite-free and in good health.

Evaluation is somewhat more complicated in the Collie puppy. The PennHip™ procedure can determine risk for developing hip dysplasia in pups as young as 16 weeks of age. For pups younger than that, you should request copies of OFA or GDC registration for both parents. If the parents haven't both been registered, their hip and elbow status should be considered unknown and questionable.

Because eye problems in Collies are unfortunately so common, the veterinarian must examine the dog's eyes thoroughly.

All Collies, regardless of age, should be screened for evidence of von Willebrand's disease. This can be accomplished with a simple blood test. The incidence is high enough in the breed that there is no excuse for not performing the test.

For animals older than one year of age, your veterinarian will also want to take a blood sample to check for thyroid function in addition to von Willebrand's disease. A heartworm test, urinalysis and evaluation of feces for internal parasites is also indicated. If there are any patches of hair loss, a skin scraping should be taken to determine if the dog has evidence of demodectic mange.

Your veterinarian should also perform a very thorough ophthalmologic (eye) examination. The most common eye problems in Collies are collie eye anomaly (CEA), cataracts, and progressive retinal atrophy. It is best to acquire a pup whose parents have both been screened for heritable eye diseases and certified "clear" by organizations such as CERF. This is exceptionally important in the Collie because of the extremely high incidence of hereditary eye diseases in this breed. If both parents have been clear on annual CERF tests, an examination by your veterinarian is probably sufficient and referral to an ophthalmologist is only necessary if recommended by your veterinarian.

BEHAVIORAL SCREENING

Medical screening is important but don't forget temperament. More dogs are killed each year for behavioral reasons than

The Collie puppy should be amenable to handling. One excellent temperament test is to see how the pup responds to having his nails clipped. You can't expect 100% cooperation, but a psychotic, screaming puppy with long nails is no fun either.

for all medical problems combined. Temperament testing is a valuable although not infallible tool in the screening process. The reason that temperament is so important is that many dogs are eventually destroyed because they exhibit undesirable behaviors. Although not all behaviors are evident in young pups (e.g., aggression often takes many months to manifest itself), detecting anxious and fearful pups (and avoiding them) can be very important in the selection process. Traits most identifiable in

the young pup include: fear; excitability; low pain threshold; extreme submission; and noise sensitivity. There are many different techniques available and a complete discussion is beyond the scope of this book.

Pups can be evaluated for temperament as early as seven to eight weeks of age. Some behaviorists, breeders and trainers recommend objective testing where scores are given in several different categories. Others are more casual about the process since it only a crude indicator anyway. In general, the evalua-

A puppy that is responsive and enjoys the company of humans stands at the head of the class. This star pupil is owned by Leslie Canavan.

Observe how the pup reacts to his littermates. The puppy who's bounding with enthusiasm and not afraid to "go for it" is the one for you. Owner, Leslie Canavan.

tion takes place in three stages, by someone the pup has not been exposed to. The testing is not done within 72 hours of vaccination or surgery. First, the pup is observed and handled to determine its sociability. Puppies with obvious undesirable

How does the puppy react to strange objects like this fuzzy squeaky toy? If he's curious and fearless, you've found a winner. Don't be a loser and fall for a shy, nervous pup—play to win! Owner, Joe Koehler.

traits such as shyness, hyperactivity or uncontrollable biting may turn out to be unsuitable. Second, the desired pup is separated from the others and then observed for how it responds when played with and called. Third, the pup should be stimulated in various ways and its responses noted. Suitable activities include lying the pup on its side, grooming it, clipping its nails, gently grasping it around the muzzle and testing its reactions to noise. In a study conducted at the Psychology Department of Colorado State University, the staff also found that heart rate was a good indicator in this third stage of evaluation. Actually, they noted the resting heart rates, stimulated the pups with a loud noise and measured how long it took the heart rates to recover to resting levels. Most pups recovered within 36 seconds. Dogs that took considerably longer were more likely to be anxious.

Puppy aptitude tests (PAT) can be given in which a numerical score is given for eleven different traits, with a "1" representing the most assertive or aggressive expression of a trait and a "6" representing disinterest, independence or inaction. The traits assessed in the PAT include: social attraction to people, following, restraint, social dominance, elevation (lifting off ground by evaluator), retrieve, touch sensitivity, sound sensitivity, prey/chase drive, stability, and energy level. Although the tests do not absolutely predict behaviors, they do tend to do well at predicting puppies at behavioral extremes.

Is the puppy social? That simply means he likes humans and welcomes their overtures. At all costs—*yours!*— avoid the unsociable pup.

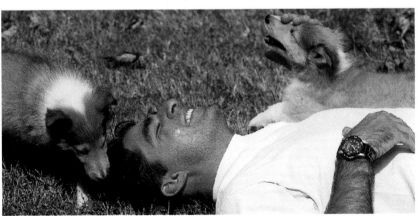

ORGANIZATIONS YOU SHOULD KNOW ABOUT

The Orthopedic Foundation for Animals (OFA) is a nonprofit organization established in 1966 to collect and disseminate information concerning orthopedic diseases of animals and to establish control programs to lower the incidence of orthopedic diseases in animals. A registry is maintained for both hip dysplasia and elbow dysplasia. The ultimate purpose of OFA cer-

Lifting the puppy off the ground to judge his reaction is a common way to evaluate temperament. The pup should remain calm and trusting without panicking or resisting.

tification is to provide information to dog owners to assist in the selection of good breeding animals; therefore, attempts to get a dysplastic dog certified will only hurt the breed by perpetuation of the disease. For more information contact your veterinarian or the Orthopedic Foundation for Animals, 2300 Nifong Blvd., Columbia, MO 65201.

The Institute for Genetic Disease Control in Animals (GDC) is a nonprofit organization founded in 1990. It maintains an open registry for orthopedic problems but does not compete with OFA. In an open registry like GDC, owners, breeders, veterinarians, and scientists can trace the genetic history of any particular dog once that dog and close relatives have been registered. At the present time, the GDC operates open registries for hip dysplasia, elbow dysplasia, and osteochondrosis. The GDC is currently developing guidelines for registries of Legg-Calve-Perthes disease, craniomandibular osteopathy, and medial patellar luxation. For more information, contact the Institute for Genetic Disease Control in Animals, P.O. Box 222, Davis, CA 95617.

The Canine Eye Registration Foundation (CERF) is an international organization devoted to eliminating hereditary eye diseases from purebred dogs. This organization is similar to OFA, which helps eliminate diseases like hip dysplasia. CERF is a nonprofit organization that screens and certifies purebreds as free of heritable eye diseases. Dogs are **Your Collie pup starts out with an advantage in life if he comes from healthy parents that are certified as free of genetic disease.**

evaluated by veterinary eye specialists and findings are then submitted to CERF for documentation. The goal is to identify purebreds without heritable eye problems so they can be used for breeding. Dogs being considered for breeding programs should be screened and certified by CERF on an annual basis since not all problems are evident in puppies. For more information on CERF, write to CERF, SCC-A, Purdue University, West Lafayette, IN 47907.

Project TEACH™ (Training and Education in Animal Care and Health) is a voluntary accreditation process for those individuals selling animals to the public. It is administered by Pet Health Initiative, Inc. (PHI) and provides instruction on genetic screening as well as many other aspects of proper pet care. TEACH-accredited sources screen animals for a variety of medical, behavioral and infectious diseases *before* they are sold. Project TEACH™ supports the efforts of registries such as OFA, GDC and CERF and recommends that all animals sold be registered with the appropriate agencies. For more information on Project TEACH™, send a self-addressed stamped envelope to Pet Health Initiative, P.O. Box 12093, Scottsdale, AZ 85267-2093.

A dream from Sweden: this is Zigline's Silver Dream in Blue owned by Monica Lonnstrom.

FEEDING & NUTRITION

WHAT YOU MUST CONSIDER EVERY DAY TO FEED YOUR COLLIE THROUGH HIS LIFETIME

Nutrition is one of the most important aspects of raising a healthy Collie and yet it is often the source of much controversy between breeders, veterinarians, pet owners and dog food manufacturers. However, most of these arguments have more to do more with

Facing page: Many breeders recommend supplementing your Collie's food with fresh vegetables, meats and fruits. While many commercial foods are "balanced," they cannot offer your dog everything he needs. Owner, Leslie Canavan.

marketing than with science. Let's first take a look at dog foods and then determine the needs of our dog. This chapter will concentrate of feeding the pet Collie rather than breeding or working animals.

COMMERCIAL DOG FOODS

Most dog foods are sold based on marketing (i.e., how to make a product appealing to owners while meeting the needs of dogs). Some foods are marketed on the basis of their protein content; others based on a "special" ingredient; and some are sold because they don't contain certain ingredients (e.g., preservatives, soy). We want a dog food that specifically meets our dog's needs, is economical and causes few, if any, problems. Most foods come in dry, semi-moist and canned forms. Some can now be purchased frozen. The "dry" foods are the most economical, and contain the least fat and the most preservatives. The canned foods are the most expensive (they're 75% water), usually contain the most fat, and have the least preservatives. Semi-moist foods are expensive, high in sugar content and I do not recommend them for any dogs.

The nutritional needs of each puppy are different. Observing the puppy carefully through each of his developmental stages can tell you much about his dietary needs.

Puppyhood is the most important time to pay attention to what your Collie needs. While he is growing quickly, his body needs complete nutrition and you need to understand how to provide it.

When you're selecting a commercial diet, make sure the food has been assessed by feeding trials for a specific life stage, not just by nutrient analysis. This statement is usually located not far from the ingredient label. In the United States, these trials are performed in accordance with American Association of Feed Control Officials (AAFCO) and, in Canada, by the Canadian Veterinary Medical Association. This certification is important because it has been found that dog foods currently on the market that provide only a chemical analysis and calculated values but no feeding trial may not provide adequate nutrition. The feeding trials show that the diets meet minimal, not optimal standards. However, they are the best tests we currently have.

PUPPY REQUIREMENTS

Soon after pups are born, and certainly within the first 24 hours, they should begin nursing their mother. This provides them with colostrum, which is an antibody-rich milk that helps protect them from infection for their first few months of life. Pups should be allowed to nurse

A puppy can become finicky after he leaves his littermates. Mealtime with a litter is competitive and exciting. You may need to encourage a pup to eat if he loses interest. Make mealtime fun like mom did!

for at least six weeks before they are completely weaned from their mother. Supplemental feeding may be started by as early as three weeks of age.

By two months of age, pups should be fed puppy food. They are now in an important growth phase. Nutritional deficiencies and/or imbalances during this time of life are more devastating than at any other time. Also, this is not the time to overfeed pups or provide them with "performance" rations. Overfeeding Collies can lead to serious skeletal defects such as osteochondrosis, cervical vertebral instability and hip dysplasia.

Pups should be fed "growth" diets until they are 12–18 months of age. Many Collies do not mature until 18 months of age and so benefit from a longer period on these rations. Pups will initially need to be fed two to three meals daily until they are 12–18 months old, then once to twice daily (preferably twice) when they are converted to adult food. Proper growth diets should be selected based on acceptable feeding trials designed for growing pups. If you can't tell by reading the label, ask your veterinarian for feeding advice.

Remember that pups need "balance" in their diets and

avoid the temptation to supplement with protein, vitamins, or minerals. Calcium supplements have been implicated as a cause of bone and cartilage deformity, especially in large-breed puppies. Puppy diets are already heavily fortified with calcium, and supplements tend to unbalance the mineral intake. There is more than adequate proof that these supplements are responsible for many bone deformities seen in these growing dogs.

ADULT DIETS

The goal of feeding adult dogs is one of "maintenance." They have already done the growing they are going to do and are unlikely to have the digestive problems of elderly dogs. In general, dogs can do well on maintenance rations containing predominantly plant or animal-based ingredients as long as that ration has been specifically formulated to meet maintenance-level requirements. This contention should be supported by studies performed by the manufacturer in accordance with AAFCO (American Association of Feed Control Officials). In Canada, these products should be certified by the Canadian Veterinary Medical Association to meet maintenance requirements.

Oscar is trying to tell us that puppies require fresh water and lots of it, especially on summer days. This thirsty three-month-old is owned by Louise Gordon.

There's nothing wrong with feeding a cereal-based diet to a dog on maintenance rations, and this is the most economical. When comparing maintenance rations, it must be appreciated that these diets must meet the "minimum" requirements for confined dogs, not necessarily optimal levels. Most dogs will benefit when fed diets that contain easily digested ingredients that provide nutrients at least slightly above minimum requirements. Typically, these foods will be intermediate in price between the most expensive super-premium diets and the cheapest generic diets. Select only those diets that have been substantiated by feeding trials to meet maintenance requirements, those that contain wholesome ingredients, and those recommended by your veterinarian. Don't select based on price alone, on company advertising, or on total protein content.

GERIATRIC DIETS

Collies are considered elderly when they are about seven years of age, and there are certain changes that occur as dogs age that alter their nutritional requirements. As pets age, their metabolism slows and this must be accounted for. If maintenance

As your Collie's metabolism slows down, the amount you feed should decrease as well. Overfeeding a less active dog results in unnecessary weight gain, which is a curse at any age.

rations are fed in the same amounts while metabolism is slowing, weight gain may result. Obesity is the last thing one wants to contend with in an elderly pet, since it increases the risk of several other health-related problems. As pets age, most of their organs function not as well as in youth. The digestive system, the liver, pancreas and

is to minimize the potential damage done by taking this into account while the dog is still well. If we wait until an elderly dog is ill before we change the diet, we have a much harder job.

Elderly dogs need to be treated as individuals. While some benefit from the nutrition found in "senior" diets, others might do better on the highly digestible

The Carrot Bone® from Nylabone® is a completely edible and wonderfully enticing treat for dogs. It not only provides vegetable protein and goodness but it also helps clean your Collie's teeth.

gallbladder are not functioning at peak effect. The intestines have more difficulty extracting all the nutrients from the food consumed. A gradual decline in kidney function is considered a normal part of aging.

A responsible approach to geriatric nutrition is to realize that degenerative changes are a normal part of aging. Our goal

puppy and super-premium diets. These latter diets provide an excellent blend of digestibility and amino acid content but, unfortunately, many are higher in salt and phosphorus than the older pet really needs.

Older dogs are also more prone to developing arthritis and therefore it is important not to overfeed them since obesity puts added stress on the joints. For animals with joint pain, supplementing the diet with fatty acid combinations containing cis-linoleic acid, gamma-linolenic acid and eicosapentaenoic acid can be quite beneficial.

MEDICAL CONDITIONS AND DIET

It is important to keep in mind that dietary choices can affect the development of orthopedic diseases such as hip dysplasia and osteochondrosis. When feeding a pup at risk, avoid high-calorie diets and try to feed several times a day rather than ad libitum. Sudden growth spurts are to be avoided because they result in joint instability. Recent research has also suggested that the electrolyte balance of the diet may also play a role in the development of hip dysplasia. Rations that had more balance between the positively and negatively charged elements in the diet (e.g., sodium, potassium, chloride) were less likely to promote hip dysplasia in susceptible dogs. Also avoid supplements of calcium, phosphorus and vitamin D as they can interfere with normal bone and cartilage development. The fact is that calcium levels in the body are carefully regulated by hormones (such as calcitonin and

parathormone) as well as vitamin D. Supplementation disturbs this normal regulation and can cause many problems. It has also been shown that calcium supplementation can interfere with the proper absorption of zinc from the intestines. If you really feel the need to supplement your dog, select products such as eicosapentaenoic/gamma-linolenic fatty acid combinations or small amounts of vitamin C.

Diet can't prevent bloat (gastric dilatation-volvulus), but changing feeding habits can make a difference. Initially, the bloat occurs when the stomach becomes distended with swallowed air. This air is swallowed as a consequence of gulping food or water, stress and exercising too close to mealtime. This is where we can make a difference. Divide meals and feed them three times daily rather than all at once. Soak dry dog food in water before feeding to decrease the tendency to gulp the food. If you want to feed dry food only, add some large, clean chew toys to the feed bowl so that the dog has to "pick" to get at the food and can't gulp it. Putting the food bowl on a step-stool so the dog doesn't have to stretch to get the food may also be helpful. Finally, don't allow any exercise for at least one hour before and after feeding.

Fat supplements are probably the most common supplements purchased from pet supply stores. They frequently promise to add luster, gloss, and sheen to the coat, and consequently make dogs look healthy. The only fatty acid that is essential for this purpose is cis-linoleic acid, which is found in flaxseed oil, sunflower seed oil, and safflower oil. Corn oil is a suitable but less effective alternative. Most of the other oils found in retail supplements are high in saturated and monounsaturated fats and are not beneficial for shiny fur or healthy skin. For dogs with aller-gies, arthritis, high blood pressure (hypertension), high cholesterol, and some heart ailments, other fatty acids may be prescribed by a veterinarian. The important ingredients in these products are gamma-linolenic acid (GLA), eicosapentaenoic acid (EPA), and docosa-hexaenoic acid (DHA). These products have gentle and natural anti-inflammatory properties. But don't be fooled by imitations. Most retail fatty acid supplements do not contain these functional forms of the essential fatty acids—look for gamma-linolenic acid, eicosa-pentaenoic acid, and docosa-hexaenoic acid on the label.

Table manners do not figure into the good eating habits of your Collie. Owner, Leslie Canavan.

Health

**PREVENTIVE MEDICINE AND HEALTH CARE
FOR YOUR COLLIE**

Keeping your Collie healthy requires preventive health care. This is not only the most effective but the least expensive way to battle ill-ness. Good preventive care starts even before puppies are born. The dam should be well cared for, vaccinated and free of infections and parasites.

Facing page: Your goal as the owner of a smiling Collie puppy is to maintain his vitality and keep his spirits glowing for all his days.

Hopefully, both parents were screened for important genetic diseases, registered with the appropriate agencies (e.g., OFA, GDC, CERF), showed no evidence of medical or behavioral problems and were found to be good candidates for breeding. This gives the pup a good start in life. If all has been planned well, the dam will pass on resistance to disease to her pups that will last for the first few months of life. However, the dam can also pass on parasites, infections, genetic diseases and more.

TWO TO THREE WEEKS OF AGE

By two to three weeks of life, it is usually necessary to start pups on a regimen to control worms. Although dogs benefit from this parasite control, the primary reason for doing this is human health. After whelping, the dam often sheds large numbers of worms even if she tested negative previously. This is because many worms lay dormant in tissues and the stress of delivery causes parasite release and shedding into the environment. As-

Young puppies should be plump and well coated. You can't tell much else about a puppy and his future health from just looking at him—you must rely on the breeder's screening to best ensure the health of your chosen pup.

sume that all puppies potentially have worms because studies have shown that 75% do. Thus, we institute worm control early to protect the people in the house from worms, more than the pups themselves. The deworming is repeated every two to three weeks until your veterinarian feels the condition is under control. Nursing bitches should be treated at the same time because they often shed worms during this time. Only use products recommended by your veterinarian. Over-the-counter parasiticides have been responsible for deaths in pups.

By ten weeks of age, the puppy has already received his first set of vaccinations. Breeders do not permit pups to meet other dogs before they are pro perly vaccinated. Owner, Larry Stevick.

SIX TO TWENTY WEEKS OF AGE

Most puppies are weaned from their mother at six to eight weeks of age. Weaning shouldn't be done too early so that pups have the opportunity to socialize with their littermates and dam. This is important for them to be able to respond to other dogs later in life. There is no reason to rush the weaning process unless the dam can't produce enough milk to feed the pups.

Pups are usually first examined by their veterinarian at six to eight weeks of age, which is when most vaccination schedules commence. If pups are exposed to many other dogs at this young age, veterinar-

A Collie puppy must exhibit both type and temperament, and type is more predictable than temperament. However, a sound disposition is far more important than any other breed characteristics. Owners, Pattie and Jerry Fitzgerald.

ians often opt for vaccinating with inactivated parvovirus at six weeks of age. When exposure isn't a factor, most veterinarians would rather wait to see the pup at eight weeks of age. At this point, they can also do a preliminary dental evaluation to see that all the puppy teeth are coming in correctly, check to see that the testicles are properly descending in males and that there are no health reasons to prohibit vaccination at this time. Heart murmurs, wandering knee-caps (luxating patellae), juvenile cataracts and her-

nias are usually evident by this time.

Your veterinarian may also be able to perform temperament testing on the pup by eight weeks of age, or recommend someone to do it for you. Although temperament testing is not completely accurate, it can often predict which pups are most anxious and fearful. Some form of temperament evaluation is important because behavioral problems account for more animals being euthanized (killed) each year than all medical conditions combined.

Recently, some veterinary hospitals have been recommending neutering pups as early as six to eight weeks of age. A study done at the University of Florida College of Veterinary Medicine over a span of more than four years concluded there was no increase in complications when animals were neutered when less than six months of age. The evaluators also concluded that the surgery appeared to be less stressful when done in young pups.

Most vaccination schedules consist of injections being given at 6–8, 10–12 and 14–16 weeks of age. Ideally, vaccines should not be given closer than two weeks apart and three to four weeks seems to be optimal. Each vaccine usually consists of several different viruses (e.g., parvovirus, distemper, parainfluenza, hepatitis) combined into one injection. Coronavirus can be given as a separate vaccination according to this same schedule if pups are at risk. Some veterinarians and breeders advise another parvovirus booster at 18–20 weeks of age. A booster is given for all vaccines at one year of age and annually thereafter. For animals at increased risk of exposure, parvovirus vaccination may be given as often

The docile, agreeable nature of the Collie pup is evident in these two youngsters. A long day of play and outdoor fun takes a lot out of a puppy.

as four times a year. A new vaccine for canine cough (tracheobronchitis) is squirted into the nostrils. It can be given as early as six weeks of age if pups are at risk. Leptospirosis vaccination is given in some geographic areas and likely offers protection for six to eight months. The initial series consists of three to four injections spaced two to three weeks apart, starting as early as ten weeks of age. Rabies vaccine is given as a separate injection at three months of age, then repeated when the pup is one year old, then every one to three years depending on local risk and government regulation.

Some dogs have difficulty mounting a complete and protective response to vaccinations. This is especially common in Collies but might be seen in some pups that fail to thrive and in those with cyclic hematopoiesis. In the former, we typically recommend running a test to measure antibody titer (level) for parvovirus at 16 weeks of age and annually thereafter. This helps ensure that the vaccinations that are given will, in fact, be protective.

Between 8 and 14 weeks of age, use every opportunity to expose the pup to as many people and situations as possible. This is part of the critical socialization period that will determine how good a pet your dog will become. This is not the time to abandon a puppy for eight hours while you go to work. This is also not the time to punish your dog in any way, shape or form.

This is the time to introduce your dog to neighborhood cats, birds and other creatures. Hold off on exposure to other dogs until after the second vaccination in the series. You don't want your new friend to pick up contagious diseases from dogs it meets in its travels before it has adequate protection. By 12 weeks of age, your pup should be ready for social outings with other dogs. Do them—they're a great way for your dog to feel comfortable around members of its own species. Walk the streets and introduce your pup to everybody you meet. Your goal should be to introduce your dog to every type of person or situation it is likely to encounter in its life. Take it in cars, elevators, buses, travel crates, subways, parade grounds, beaches; you want it to habituate to all environments. Expose your pup to kids, teenagers, old people, people in wheelchairs, people on bicycles, and people in uniforms. The more varied the exposure, the better the socialization.

The microchip, one modern way to identify your dog, is injected under the dog's skin and can be scanned for positive identification. The chip is no larger than a grain of rice.

Proper identification of your pet is also important since this minimizes the risk of theft and increases the chances that your pet will be returned to you if it is lost. There are several different options. Microchip implantation is a relatively painless procedure involving the subcutaneous injection of an implant the size of a grain of rice. This implant does not act as a beacon if your pet goes missing. However, if your pet turns up at a veterinary clinic or shelter and is checked with a scanner, the chip provides information about the owner that can be used to quickly reunite you with your pet. This method of identification is reasonably priced, permanent in nature, and performed at most veterinary clinics. Another option is tattooing, which can be done on the inner ear or on the skin of the abdomen. Most purebreds are given a number by the associated registry (e.g., American Kennel Club, United Kennel Club, Canadian Kennel Club,

The skin of the abdomen is the best area to tattoo your Collie. Tattooing has become fairly common among purebred dogs and is recommended by most breeders and veterinarians.

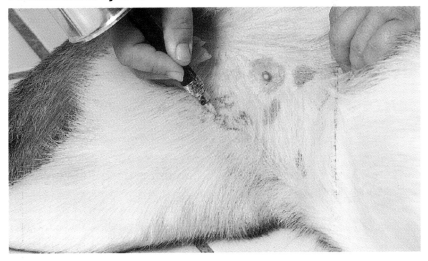

The Collie is an athletic purebred dog that thrives on activity and challenge. Fortunately, Collie breeders have screened breed members carefully for orthopedic diseases so that Collies continue to enjoy strong hips and elbows.

etc.) and this is used for identification. Alternatively, permanent numbers such as social security numbers (telephone numbers and addresses may change during the life of your pet) can be used in the tattooing process. There are several different tattoo registries maintaining lists of dogs, their tattoo codes and their owners. Finally, identifying collars and tags provide quick information but can be separated from your pet if it is lost of stolen. They work best when combined with a permanent identification system such as microchip implantation or tattooing.

FOUR TO TWELVE MONTHS OF AGE

At 16 weeks of age, when your pup gets the last in its series of regular induction vaccinations, ask your veterinarian about evaluating the pup for hip dysplasia with the PennHip™ technique. This helps predict the risk of developing hip dysplasia as well as degenerative joint disease. Collie breeders have done an excellent job decreasing the incidence of hip dysplasia through routine screening and registration programs. Since anesthesia is typically required for the procedure, many veterinarians like to do the evaluation at the same time as neutering.

At this same time, it is very worthwhile to perform a diagnostic test for von Willebrand's disease, an inherited disorder that causes uncontrolled bleeding. This trait is not uncommon in the Collie. A simple blood test is all that is required, but it may need to be sent to a special laboratory to have the test performed. You will be extremely happy you had the foresight to have this done before neutering. If your dog does have a bleeding problem, it will be necessary to take special precautions during surgery.

As a general rule, neuter your animal at about six months of age unless you fully intend to breed it. As mentioned earlier, neutering can be safely done at eight weeks of age, but this is still not a common practice. Neutering not only stops the possibility of pregnancy and undesirable behaviors, but can prevent several health problems as well. It is a well-established fact that pups spayed before their first heat have a dramatically reduced incidence of mammary (breast) cancer. Neutered males significantly decrease their incidence of prostate disorders.

Also when your pet is six months of age, your veterinarian will want to take a blood sample to perform a heartworm test. If the test is negative and shows no evidence of heartworm infection, the pup will go on heartworm prevention therapy. Some veterinarians are even recommending preventive therapy in younger pups. This might be a one-a-day regimen, but newer therapies can be given on a once-a-month basis. As a bonus, most of these heartworm preventatives also help prevent internal parasites.

If your Collie has any patches of hair loss, your veterinarian will want to perform a skin scraping with a scalpel blade to see if any *Demodex* mites are responsible. If there is a problem, don't lose hope; about 90% of demodicosis cases can be cured with supportive care only. However, it's important to diagnose it early before scarring results.

Another part of the six-month visit should be a thorough dental evaluation to make sure all the permanent teeth have correctly erupted. If they haven't, this will be the time to correct the problem. Correction should only be performed to make the animal more comfortable and promote more normal chewing. The procedures should never be used to cosmetically improve the appearance of a dog used for show purposes or breeding.

After the dental evaluation, you should start implementing home dental care. In most cases, this will consist of brushing the teeth one or more times each week and perhaps using dental rinses. It is a sad fact that 85% of dogs over four years of age have periodontal disease and doggy breath. In fact it is so common that most people think it is "normal." Well, it is normal — as normal as bad breath would be in people if they never brushed their teeth. Brush your dog's teeth regularly with a special tooth brush and toothpaste and you can greatly reduce the incidence of tartar buildup, bad breath and gum disease. Better preventive care means that dogs live a long time. They'll enjoy their sunset years more if they still have their teeth. Ask your veterinarian for details on home dental care.

Nylabones® and Gumabones® help ensure clean teeth and gums and better breath. Veterinarians recommend Nylabones® for all their patients, from puppyhood through senior years. Nylabone® is the only chew device accepted by the American Veterinary Medical Association for advertising in its official *Journal*.

Just say "Ahhh"! Don't take your Collie's health for granted—especially his teeth.

Your veterinarian will regularly check your Collie's eyes for signs of cloudiness or other indications of possible developing conditions.

ONE TO SEVEN YEARS OF AGE

At one year of age, your dog should be re-examined and have boosters for all vaccines. Your veterinarian will also want to do a very thorough physical examination to look for early evidence of problems. This might include taking radiographs (x-rays) of the hips and elbows to look for evidence of dysplastic changes. Genetic Disease Control (GDC) will certify hips and elbows at 12 months of age; Orthopedic Foundation for Animals won't issue certification until 24 months of age.

At 12 months of age, it's also a great time to have some blood samples analyzed to provide

Examining the gums and teeth of the Collie on a regular basis can help an owner know how well he's doing at warding off gum diseases and tooth loss.

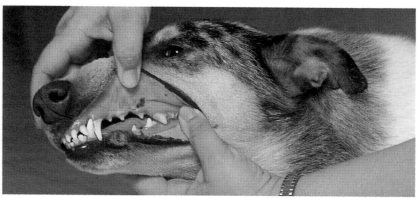

If your veterinarian's exam of your Collie isn't thorough enough, don't hesitate to ask questions. If you're not satisfied, seek out a new veterinarian. Here, Dr. Henry gives Shamrock Sage Brush Nite Sky a thorough exam. Owners, Pattie and Jerry Fitzgerald.

background information. Although few Collies experience clinical hypothyroidism at this young age, the process may be starting. Therefore, it is a good idea to have baseline levels of thyroid hormones (free and total), TSH (thyroid-stimulating hormone), blood cell counts, organ chemistries and cholesterol levels. This can serve as a valuable comparison to samples collected in the future.

Each year, preferably around the time of your pet's birthday, it's time for another veterinary visit. This visit is a wonderful opportunity for a thorough clinical examination rather than just "shots." Since 85% of dogs have periodontal disease by four years of age, veterinary intervention does not seem to be as widespread as it should be. The examination should include visually inspecting the ears, eyes (a great time to start scrutinizing for progressive retinal atrophy, cataracts, etc.), mouth (don't wait for gum disease), and groin; listening (auscultation) to the lungs and heart; feeling (palpating) the lymph nodes and abdomen; and answering all of your questions about optimal health care. In addition, booster

55

vaccinations are given during these times, feces are checked for parasites, urine is analyzed and blood samples may be collected for analysis. One of the tests run on the blood sample is for heartworm antigen. In areas of the country where heartworm is only present in the spring, summer and fall (it's spread by mosquitoes), blood samples are collected and evaluated about a month prior to the mosquito season. Other routine blood tests are for blood cells (hematology), organ chemistries, thyroid levels and electrolytes.

By two years of age, most veterinarians prefer to begin preventive dental cleanings, often referred to as "prophies." Anesthesia is required, and the veterinarian or veterinary dentist will use an ultrasonic scaler to remove plaque and tartar from above and below the gum line and polish the teeth so that plaque has a harder time sticking to the teeth. Radiographs (x-rays) and fluoride treatments are other options. It is now known that it is plaque, not tartar, that initiates inflammation in the gums. Since scaling and root planing remove more tartar than plaque, veterinary dentists have begun using a new technique called PerioBUD (Periodontal Bactericidal Ultrasonic Debridement). The ultrasonic treatment is quicker, disrupts more bacteria and is less irritating to the gums. With tooth polishing to finish up the procedure, gum healing is better and owners can start home care sooner. Each dog has its own dental needs that must be addressed, but most veterinary dentists recommend prophies annually.

Roar-Hide® from Nylabone® is the only molded rawhide product available. It's safe for Collies and, unlike other rawhide products, is 86.2% protein and 100% digestible.

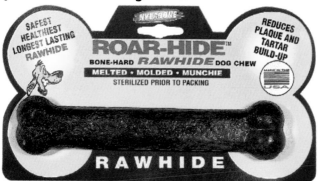

Don't neglect your old friend's health. He's depending on you most during his golden years. This is Twin Creeks Jackpot, owned by Ann Schaefer, spending time with a young friend.

SENIOR COLLIES

Collies are considered seniors when they reach about seven years of age. Veterinarians still usually only need to examine them once a year, but it is now important to start screening for geriatric problems. Accordingly blood profiles, urinalysis, chest radiographs (x-rays) and electrocardiograms (EKG) are recommended on an annual basis. When problems are caught early, they are much more likely to be successfully managed. This is as true in canine medicine as it is in human medicine.

MEDICAL PROBLEMS

**RECOGNIZED GENETIC CONDITIONS
SPECIFICALLY RELATED TO THE COLLIE**

Many conditions appear to be especially prominent in Collies. Sometimes it is possible to identify the genetic basis of a problem, but in many cases we must be satisfied with merely identifying the breeds that are at risk and how the conditions can be identified, treated and prevented. Following

Facing page: Collies are not like other purebred dogs. It's best to know the problems that specifically affect the breed so that you can best deal with them. This is Kinian owned by Lu Anne Novello.

are some conditions that have been recognized as being common in the Collie, but this listing is certainly not complete. Also, many genetic conditions may be common in certain breed lines, not in the breed in general.

CATARACTS

Cataracts refer to an opacity or cloudiness on the lens, and ophthalmologists are careful to categorize them on the basis of stage, age of onset, and location. In Collies, the exact genetics of inheritance of cataracts are not fully known. The cataracts are usually evident quite early, often in young pups but almost always before one year of age. Their location may be nuclear or cortical and associated with other eye problems such as microphthalmia (small eye), retinal dysplasia and coloboma. Many dogs adapt well to cataracts, but cataract removal surgery is available and quite successful if needed. Affected animals and their siblings should obviously not be used for breeding, and careful ophthalmologic evaluation of both parents is warranted.

COLLIE EYE ANOMALY

Collie Eye Anomaly (CEA) is the incomplete development of the eye and is inherited as a simple recessive defect, but a cluster of genes controls the severity and susceptibility. That's how there can be such variability in pups from the same litter. Most collies (80–90%) with CEA don't have vision problems, but some can have very serious hemorrhages within the eye and large defects of the optic nerve (colobomas). The condition is not fatal but can result in blindness.

Since the condition is present at birth, pups can be checked as early as five to six weeks of age, although six to ten weeks of age is preferred. The biggest problems are that carriers can't be detected by any known diagnostic tests, including examination with an ophthalmoscope. This is significant because some estimates cite that 90% of Collies may be carriers for the trait. Diagnosis of the condition in merle-colored Collies can be quite difficult. There is no treatment for Collie Eye Anomaly.

The best form of prevention is to register all pups with the Canine Eye Registration Foundation (CERF) and only purchase pups from parents that have been registered. Only normal-eyed Collies should be used for breeding. Mildly affected pups (grade one or two) can still make acceptable pets but their parents are definite "carriers" and should not be used for further breeding.

CYCLIC HEMATOPOIESIS (GRAY COLLIE SYNDROME)

Some Collie pups born with a silver-gray haircoat may be smaller and weaker than their normal littermates, and may have light-colored noses. This condition appears to be transmitted as an autosomal recessive trait. By 8–12 weeks of age, affected pups start to develop problems such as fever, diarrhea, eye infections, painful joints (arthralgia) and abnormalities of their white blood cells.

When blood samples are collected daily over a two-week period, it can be seen that the neutrophils, a type of white blood cell, fluctuate from high to low over an 11–14 day cycle. When the neutrophils are at their lowest point, these pups are very susceptible to overwhelming infection and usually die during these periods.

Diagnosis can be confirmed by sequential blood counts over a 14-day period. Therapy is invariably unsuccessful and most animals succumb during periods of low neutrophil counts. Parents and littermates should not be used for breeding.

DEMODICOSIS

Demodex mites are present on the skin of all dogs, but in some animals born with a defective immune system the numbers increase and begin to cause problems. Collies are usually cited as one of the most common breeds affected with this condition. Although it is thought to be genetically transmitted, the mode of transmission has never been conclusively demonstrated.

The *Demodex* mite is cigar shaped and can be easily detected with a microscope.

Most cases of demodicosis are seen in young pups and fully 90% of cases self-cure with little or no medical intervention by the time these dogs reach immunologic maturity at 18–36 months of age. In these cases, it is suspected that the immune system is marginally compromised and eventually matures and gets the condition under control. On the other hand, some pups (about 10% of those initially affected) do not get better and, in fact, become progressively worse. These are thought to have more severe immunologic compromise and are often labeled as having "generalized demodicosis."

The diagnosis is easily made by scraping the skin with a scalpel blade and looking at the collected debris under a microscope. The *Demodex* mites are cigar-shaped and are easily seen. What is harder to identify is the immunologic defect that allowed the condition to occur in the first place. Recent research has suggested the problem may be linked to a decrease in interleukin-2 response, but the genetics is still a question.

If the cause of the immune dysfunction can be cured, the mange will resolve on its own. Likewise, if the pup outgrows its immunologic immaturity or de-

fect, the condition will self-cure. This process can best be assisted by ensuring a healthy diet is being fed, treating for any internal parasites or other diseases, and perhaps using cleansing shampoos and nutritional supplements that help bolster the immune system. However, if the condition does not resolve on its own, or if it is getting worse despite conservative therapy, special mite-killing treatments are necessary. Amitraz is the most common dip used, but experimentally, milbemycin oxime and ivermectin given daily have shown some promising results. Please remember that some Collies are extremely sensitive to the adverse effects of ivermectin. At the doses recommended to treat demodicosis, a susceptible Collie could have a fatal reaction. Consider all alternatives before using ivermectin in this breed. It must be remembered that killing the mites will not restore the immune system to normal.

Regarding prevention, it is best not to breed dogs with a history of demodicosis, and dogs with generalized demodicosis should *never* be bred. Although the genetic nature of this disease has not been decisively proven, it doesn't make sense to add affected individuals to the gene pool of future generations.

DERMATOMYOSITIS

Dermatomyositis is seen most commonly in the Collie and is a disease that affects skin and muscle. The exact cause of the disorder is still a matter of debate. It is known to involve the immune system and likely has hereditary (and possibly infectious) components.

Animals first begin to show signs at about 12 weeks of age that may look like scrapes on the face, ears, elbows, hocks and other friction points. Hair may also be lost from the tip of the tail. In later stages, muscle wasting may also be seen, especially on the top of the head (temporalis muscles) and over the hindquarters.

The condition is inherited as an autosomal dominant trait with variable expressivity. This means that if one parent is affected, most of the pups will be affected. There is also speculation that a virus may be involved in the condition. It is thought that a virus could induce clinical signs typical of the disease in genetically predisposed dogs. This then initiates an immune-mediated (autoimmune) form of skin disease. Diagnosis is made by skin biopsy or by electromyograms.

Therapy is only symptomatic. Both vitamin E and corticoster-

Early manifestations of dermatomyositis. Courtesy of Dr. Thomas Lewis, Dermatology Clinic for Animals, Albuquerque, New Mexico.

oids have been used to relieve scaling and scarring, but neither will cure the condition. Pentoxifylline is currently being investigated experimentally to see if it holds any promise for the treatment of dermatomyositis. Recovered animals should definitely not be bred, since offspring will undoubtedly be affected, at least to some extent. It is risky to use siblings or parents in future breedings. The Collie Club of America Foundation supports research for gene identification of carriers of dermatomyositis. The first stage

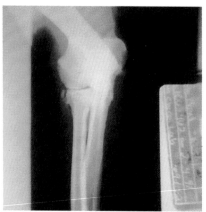

Elbow dysplasia radiographs are submitted to a registry for evaluation.

of gene sequencing has been done and it is estimated that over 70% of Collies have variants of this disease or are affected as carriers.

ELBOW DYSPLASIA

Elbow dysplasia doesn't refer to just one disease, but rather an entire complex of disorders that affect the elbow joint. The good news is that elbow dysplasia isn't very common in the Collie. However, since the incidence is so low, continued registration is recommended because it should be possible to completely eliminate the condition in Collies by conscientious breeding.

Radiographs (x-rays) are taken of the elbow joints and submitted to a registry for evaluation, such as The Orthopedic Foundation for Animals (OFA)

or Genetic Disease Control in Animals (GDC). Only animals with "normal" elbows should be used for breeding.

HIP DYSPLASIA

Hip dysplasia is a genetically transmitted developmental problem of the hip joint that is common in many breeds. Fortunately, it is relatively rare in the Collie. Based on research tabulated up to January, 1995, the Orthopedic Foundation for Animals concluded that 3.2% of the radiographs submitted from Collies had evidence of hip dysplasia. This is great news because the Collie breeders have been able to reduce the incidence in the breed by 50–60% just through conscientious breeding.

When purchasing a Collie pup, it is best to ensure that the parents were both registered with normal hips through one of the international registries such as the Orthopedic Foundation for Animals or Genetic Disease Control. Pups over 16 weeks of age can be tested by veterinarians trained in the PennHip™ procedure, which is a way of predicting risk of developing hip dysplasia and arthritis. In time it should be possible to completely eradicate hip dysplasia from the breed.

HYPOTHYROIDISM

Hypothyroidism is the most commonly diagnosed endocrine (hormonal) problem in the Collie. The disease itself refers to an insufficient amount of thyroid hormones being produced. Although there are several different potential causes, lymphocytic thyroiditis is by far the most common. Iodine deficiency and goiter are extremely rare. In lymphocytic thyroiditis, the body produces antibodies that target aspects of thyroid tissue; the process usually starts between one and three years of age in affected animals but doesn't become clinically evident until later in life.

There is a great deal of misinformation about hypothyroidism. Owners often expect their dog to be obese with the condition and otherwise don't suspect it. The fact is that hypothyroidism is quite variable in its manifestations, and obesity is only seen in a small percentage of cases. In most cases, affected animals appear fine until they use up most of their remaining thyroid hormone reserves. The most common manifestations then are lack of energy and recurrent infections. Hair loss is seen in about one-third of cases.

You might suspect that hypothyroidism would be easy to diagnose, but it is trickier than you think. Since there is a large reserve of thyroid hormones in the body, a test measuring only total blood levels of the hormones (T-4 and T-3) is not a very sensitive indicator of the condition. Thyroid stimulation tests are the best way to measure the functional reserve. Measuring "free" and "total" levels of the hormones or endogenous TSH (Thyroid-Stimulating Hormone) are other approaches. Also, since we know that most cases are due to antibodies produced in the body, screening for these autoantibodies can help identify animals at risk of developing hypothyroidism.

Because this breed is so prone to developing hypothyroidism, periodic "screening" for the disorder is warranted in many cases. Although none of the screening tests is perfect, a basic panel evaluating total T-4, free T-4, TSH and cholesterol levels is a good start. Ideally, this would first be performed at one year of age and annually thereafter. This "screening" is practical, because none of these tests is very expensive.

Fortunately, although there may be some problems in diagnosing hypothyroidism, treatment is straightforward and relatively inexpensive. Supplementing the affected animal twice daily with thyroid hormone effectively treats the condition. In many breeds, supplementation with thyroid hormones is commonly done to help confirm the diagnosis. Animals with hypothyroidism should not be used in a breeding program, and those with circulating autoantibodies but no actual hypothyroid disease should also not be used for breeding.

IVERMECTIN SENSITIVITY

Collies seem to be particularly sensitive to the drug ivermectin that is found in some heartworm preventatives. Not all Collies have this sensitivity, but since it is impossible to tell which ones will have problems, it is best not to use this drug in any Collies. Fortunately, there are other medications to use as heartworm preventatives (milbemycin oxime, carbamazine citrate).

In most of the studies done to date, the ivermectin didn't cause problems in doses under 50 micrograms per kilogram body weight. Since the proper dosage of the medication is 6 micrograms per kilogram, it is reasonable to assume that the dosage recommended for heartworm prevention shouldn't cause problems. However, in some cases it

does, so it is just not worth recommending the drug in any dose for use in Collies. Mildly affected Collies may have increased salivation, dilated pupils, vomiting, tremors, and difficulty walking, (ataxia) but fatal reactions have also been reported. Accordingly, it is not recommended that you experiment on your Collie to test its sensitivity to the drug. Use something else.

LUPUS ERYTHEMATOSUS

Lupus erythematosus (LE) is a disorder that occurs in dogs as well as people, and is caused by abnormal antibodies that circulate in the blood. It can cause quite widespread problems. One form of the disease affects many different organs (systemic lupus erythematosus) while the other (cutaneous or discoid lupus erythematosus) affects only the skin.

The most frequent clinical findings with systemic lupus erythematosus (SLE) are a fever that does not improve with antibiotics, arthritis, kidney disease, anemia, and skin problems, although many other disorders have been described. Collies are the most common breed affected.

Cutaneous (discoid) lupus erythematosus often causes a facial rash and has been referred to as "Collie nose." The important distinction between systemic and cutaneous lupus erythematosus is that cutaneous lupus does not involve other body systems and that the vast majority of cases of cutaneous lupus never evolve into systemic lupus erythematosus.

Specific diagnostic testing for SLE includes a variety of blood tests and biopsies; confirmation is not always a simple matter. Cases are often referred to dermatologists for appropriate diagnostic testing and treatment. The therapy for SLE must be individualized but may be attempted with medications that suppress the immune system and the production of abnormal antibodies. Unfortunately, all of these medications have potential side effects and monitoring of blood and urine samples is an important part of the treatment regimen.

The therapy of CLE (DLE) differs from that of SLE in that heavy drug doses are usually not necessary. We should aim at limiting sun exposure (which worsens but doesn't cause the problem), use vitamin E to help lessen scarring, and use relatively lower doses of medications. One of the most successful treatments involves combining tetracycline with the B vitamin,

niacinamide. This may not achieve 100% control but our primary goal is to lessen the impact of the disease and the medications allow the animal to optimize a quality lifespan. Animals with lupus should not be used for breeding.

NODULAR FASCIITIS

Nodular fasciitis was originally called fibrous histiocytoma

"Collie nose," more technically known as cutaneous or discoid lupus erythematosus, affects only the skin of the Collie.

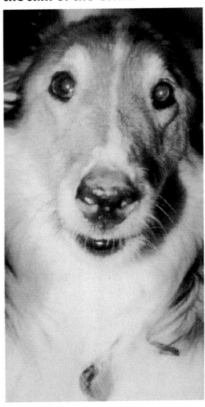

and is a tumor-like inflammatory process that involves the eyelids and lips. Dermatologists usually refer to the condition as nodular fasciitis while ophthalmologists often refer to the exact same condition as nodular (granulomatous) episcleritis. This disorder affects mainly young (two to four years of age) dogs and the Collie is certainly the most common breed implicated. The genetics of the situation are not understood and neither are the reasons for its occurrence. The diagnosis can be confirmed with biopsies. The initial treatment in most cases is injections of corticosteroids. Other immune-suppressing drugs, such as azathioprine, are also sometimes used. In some cases the condition resolves on its own, but most veterinarians find it impossible to predict the progression in any individual animal.

PATENT DUCTUS ARTERIOSUS

Patent Ductus Arteriosus (PDA) is the most common congenital heart defect seen in dogs. This is inherited as a polygenic threshold trait, which means that the trait is controlled by a number of different genes and has a threshold since clinically there can only be a hole (patency) or no hole, no clinical intermediate. This defect occurs when the normal fetal communication between the nonfunctional lungs and the aorta (major blood vessel leaving the heart) fails after birth. This results in the shunting of blood into the pulmonary artery (major vessel to the lungs) and flooding of the lungs. At the same time the rest of the body is getting an inadequate amount of circulation.

Most puppies with PDA show no clinical signs early in life, but a heart murmur is detected upon examination for first vaccination. Other puppies may develop acute heart failure and have difficulty in breathing, exercise intolerance, or develop a cough. The diagnosis of PDA is normally made by the characteristic murmur, electrocardiogram (EKG) and chest radiographs (X-rays). Surgery is needed to correct the condition. The surgery should be done as soon as possible, ideally before five months of age to minimize secondary damage to the heart and lungs. There is over a 90% success rate with the surgery, and if completed early enough, the prognosis is excellent that the dog will be able to live a normal life expectancy. If left uncorrected, the puppies usually do not live more than the first year or two.

PROGRESSIVE RETINAL ATROPHY

Progressive retinal atrophy (PRA) refers to several inherited disorders affecting the retina, which results in blindness. PRA is thought to be inherited with each breed demonstrating a specific age of onset and pattern of inheritance. In the Collie, the disease gene is *rcd 2*, the condition is inherited as an autosomal recessive trait (each parent must be a carrier for a pup to be affected) and problems start early. In fact, the retinal dysplasia starts during fetal development. There is progressive atrophy or degeneration of the retinal tissue. Visual impairment occurs slowly but progressively. Therefore, animals often adapt to their reduced vision until it is compromised to near blindness. Because of this, owners may not notice any visual impairment until the condition has progressed significantly. Rough Collies usually develop rod-cone dysplasia (Type I) and affected dogs are often night blind by six weeks of age and functionally blind by six to eight months of age.

The diagnosis of PRA can be made in two ways: direct visualization of the retina, and electroretinography (ERG). An ophthalmoscope can be used to visualize the retinal tissue at the back of the eyes. The use of indirect ophthalmoscopy requires a great deal of training and expertise and is more commonly performed by ophthalmology specialists than general practitioners. In the Collie, changes associated with PRA are usually seen by 16 weeks of age.

A highly sensitive test, usually available only from specialists, is "electroretinography," or ERG. This instrument measures electrical patterns in the retina the same way an ECG measures electrical activity of the heart. The procedure is painless, but usually available only from specialty centers. This instrument is sensitive enough to detect even the early onset of disease. In the Collie, ERG diagnosis can be made in pups by six weeks of age.

Unfortunately there is no treatment available for progressive retinal atrophy, and affected dogs eventually become blind. Identification of affected breeding animals is essential to prevent spread of the condition within the breed. Dogs from breeds at increased risk should be examined annually by a veterinary ophthalmologist. Ideally, pups should be screened at six to eight weeks of age, before being sold. The Collie Club of

America Foundation supports research for a blood test for gene-identification of PRA, which will detect carriers. Such a test is already available for Irish Setters.

SEBACEOUS ADENITIS

Sebaceous adenitis is a recently-described inflammatory disease of the hair follicles and the sebaceous glands that supply them. Most animals are in young adulthood when first affected and develop flaking of the skin and then a loss of hair. In general, the condition is not itchy or irritating unless the dogs have managed to develop infection in these sites.

Other than these changes, the dogs appear to remain in good health. For proper diagnosis, biopsies are required and they should be sent to veterinary pathologists with expertise in skin disorders. Therapy of early cases is often attempted with corticosteroids, but success is variable. Other treatments being evaluated include vitamin A derivatives (retinoids), antibiotics, cyclosporine and essential fatty acid supplements. Topical treatment is important because the skin becomes very dry and scaly. This means frequent shampooing with products that help remove surface scale (e.g. tar, salicylic acid, selenium sulfide)

and improving the moisture content of the skin with rinses of 50% propylene glycol and various other moisturizers, emollients and humectants. There is no cure and affected animals should definitely not be used for breeding.

VON WILLEBRAND'S DISEASE

Von Willebrand's disease (vWD) is the most common inherited bleeding disorder of dogs. The abnormal gene can be inherited from one or both parents. If both parents pass on the gene, most of the resultant pups fail to thrive and most will die. In most cases, though, the pup inherits a relative lack of clotting ability which is quite variable. For instance, one dog may have 15% of the clotting factor, while another might have 60%. The higher the amount, the less likely it will be that the bleeding will be readily evident since spontaneous bleeding is usually only seen when dogs have less than 30% of the normal level of von Willebrand clotting factor. Thus, some dogs don't get diagnosed until they are neutered or spayed, and they end up bleeding uncontrollably or they develop pockets of blood (hematomas) at the surgical site. In addition to the inherited form of vWD, this disorder can also be acquired in association with familial hypothyroidism. This form is usually seen in Collies older than five years of age.

Von Willebrand's disease is extremely important in the Collie because the incidence appears to be on the rise. However, there is good news. There are tests available to determine the amount of von Willebrand factor in the blood and they are accurate and reasonably priced.

Collies used for breeding should have normal amounts of von Willebrand factor in their blood, and so should all pups that are adopted as household pets. Carriers should not be used for breeding, even if they appear clinically normal. Since hypothyroidism can be linked with von Willebrand's disease, thyroid profiles can also be a useful part of the screening procedure in older Collies.

OTHER CONDITIONS COMMONLY SEEN IN THE COLLIE

- Bullous Pemphigoid
- Central Progressive Retinal Atrophy
- Cerebellar Abiotrophy (rough-coated)
- Chemodectoma
- Corneal Dystrophy
- Deafness (merle)
- Distichiasis
- Dwarfism
- Entropion
- Heterochromia Iridis
- Mandibular Distoclusion (overbite)
- Mandibular Mesioclusion (underbite)
- Microcornea
- Micropalpebral Fissure
- Microphthalmia
- Neuroaxonal Dystrophy
- Nodular Panniculitis
- Optic Nerve Hypoplasia
- Pemphigus Erythematosus
- Pemphigus Foliaceus
- Persistent Pupillary Membrane
- Posterior Crossbite
- Proliferative Episcleritis
- Retinal Dysplasia

INFECTIONS & INFESTATIONS

HOW TO PROTECT YOUR COLLIE FROM PARASITES AND MICROBES

An important part of keeping your Collie healthy is to prevent problems caused by parasites and microbes. Although there are a variety of drugs available that can help limit problems, prevention is always the desired option.

Facing page: The woods can be a scary place for your Collie. Ticks lurk in great numbers and can attach to your dog and cause problems. Always check the dog thoroughly after any romps through wooded areas.

FLEAS

Fleas are important and common parasites but not an inevitable part of every pet owner's reality. If you take the time to understand some of the basics of flea population dynamics, control is both conceivable and practical.

Fleas have four life stages (egg, larva, pupa, adult) and each stage responds to some therapies while being resistant to others. Failing to understand this is the major reason why some people have so much trouble getting the upper hand in the battle to control fleas.

Fleas spend all their time on dogs and only leave if physically removed by brushing, bathing or scratching. However, the eggs that are laid on the animal are not sticky and fall to the ground to contaminate the environment. Our goal must be to remove fleas from the animals in the house, from the house itself and from the immediate outdoor environment. Part of our plan must also involve using different medications to get rid of the different life stages as well as minimizing the use of potentially harmful insecticides that could be poisonous for pets and family members.

When de-fleaing your dog, be sure to treat his whole environment—the furniture, rugs and dog areas in the home as well as the immediate outdoor area.

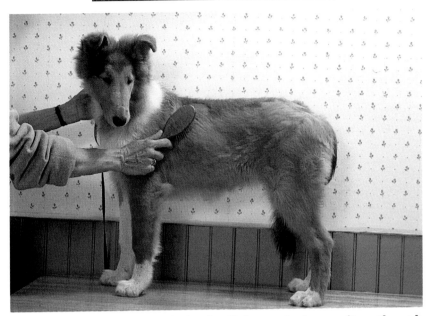

Regular grooming can help in the fight against parasites, though grooming alone will not cure a flea problem. It's either all-out war or you lose (and so does your itchy friend).

A flea comb is a very handy device for recovering fleas from pets. The best places to comb are the top of the tail, groin area, armpits, back and neck region. Fleas collected should be dropped into a container of alcohol, which quickly kills them before they can escape. In addition, all pets should be bathed with a cleansing shampoo (or flea shampoo) to remove fleas and eggs. This has no residual effect, however, and fleas can jump back on immediately after the bath if nothing else is done. Rather than using potent insecticidal dips and sprays, consider products containing the safe pyrethrins, imidacloprid or fipronil and the insect growth regulators (such as methoprene and pyripoxyfen) or insect development inhibitors (IDIs) such as lufenuron. These products are not only extremely safe, but the combination is effective against eggs, larvae and adults. This only leaves the pupal stage to cause continued problems. Insect growth regulators can also be safely given as once-a-month oral preparations. Flea collars are rarely useful, and electronic flea collars are not to be recommended for any dogs.

The initial stage of flea infestation can be rather subtle in a dog as plushly coated as a Rough Collie. Always keep an eye out whenever you're grooming or petting your dog. Owner, Angela Hungerbuhler.

To clean up the household, vacuuming is a good first step because it picks up about 50% of the flea eggs and it also stimulates flea pupae to emerge as adults, a stage when they are easier to kill with insecticides. The vacuum bag should then be removed and discarded with each treatment. Household treatment can then be initiated with pyrethrins and a combination of either insect growth regulators or sodium polyborate (a borax derivative). The pyrethrins need to be reapplied every couple of weeks, but the insect growth regulators last about two to three months and many companies guarantee sodium polyborate for a full year. Stronger insecticides such as carbamates and organophosphates can be used and will last three to four weeks in the household, but they are potentially toxic and offer no real advantages other than their persistence in the home environment. This is also one of their major disadvantages.

When an insecticide is combined with an insect growth regulator, flea control is most likely to be successful. The insecticide kills the adult fleas and the insect growth regulator affects the eggs and larvae. However, insecticides kill less than 20% of flea cocoons (pupae). Because of this, new fleas may hatch in two to three weeks despite appropriate application of products. This is known as the "pupal window" and is one of the most common causes for ineffective flea control. This is why a safe insecticide should be applied to the home environment two to three weeks after the initial treatment. This catches the newly hatched pupae before they have a chance to lay eggs and continue the flea problem.

If treatment of the outdoor environment is needed, there are several options. Pyripoxyfen, an insect growth regulator, is stable in sunlight and can be used outdoors. Sodium polyborate can be used as well, but it is important that it not be inadvertently eaten by pets. Organophosphates and carbamates are sometimes recommended for outdoor use and it is not necessary to treat the entire property. Flea control should be directed predominantly at garden margins, porches, dog houses, garages, and other pet lounging areas. Fleas don't do well with direct exposure to sunlight so generalized lawn treatment is not needed. Finally, microscopic worms (nematodes) are available that can be sprayed onto the lawn with a garden sprayer.

The nematodes eat immature flea forms and then biodegrade without harming anything else.

TICKS

Ticks are found worldwide and can cause a variety of problems, including blood loss, tick paralysis, Lyme disease, "tick fever," Rocky Mountain spotted fever and babesiosis. All are important diseases which need to be prevented whenever possible. This is only possible by limiting the exposure of our pets to ticks.

For those species of tick that dwell indoors, the eggs are laid mostly in cracks and on vertical surfaces in kennels and homes. Otherwise most other species are found outside in vegetation, such as grassy meadows, woods, brush, and weeds.

Ticks feed only on blood but they don't actually bite. They attach to an animal by sticking their harpoon-shaped mouthparts into the animal's

Vacationing in Colorado, Lu Anne Novello and her three Collies would rather not talk about Rocky Mountain spotted fever!

skin and then they suck blood. Some ticks can increase their size 20–50 times as they feed. Favorite places for them to locate are between the toes and in the ears although they can appear anywhere on the skin surface.

A good approach to prevent ticks is to remove underbrush and leaf litter, and to thin the trees in areas where dogs are allowed. This removes the cover and food sources for small mammals that serve as hosts for ticks. Ticks must have adequate cover that provides high levels of moisture and at the same time provides an opportunity of contact with animals. Keeping the lawn well maintained also makes ticks less likely to drop by and stay.

Because of the potential for ticks to transmit a variety of harmful diseases, dogs should be carefully inspected after walks through wooded areas (where ticks may be found), and careful removal of all ticks can be very important in the prevention of disease. Care should be taken not to squeeze, crush, or puncture the body of the tick, since exposure to body fluids of ticks may lead to spread of any disease carried by that tick to the animal or to the person removing the tick. The tick should be disposed of in a container of alcohol or flushed down the toilet. If the site becomes infected, veterinary attention should be sought immediately. Insecticides and repellents should only be applied to pets following appropriate veterinary advice, since indiscriminate use can be dangerous. Recently, a new tick collar has become available which contains amitraz. This collar not only kills ticks, but causes them to retract from the skin within two to three days. This greatly reduces the chances of ticks transmitting a variety of diseases. A spray formulation has also recently been developed and marketed. It might seem that there should be vaccines for all the diseases carried by ticks but only a Lyme disease (*Borrelia burgdorferi*) formulation is currently available.

MANGE

Mange refers to any skin condition caused by mites. The contagious mites include ear mites, scabies mites, *Cheyletiella* mites and chiggers. Demodectic mange is associated with proliferation of *Demodex* mites, but they are not considered contagious. Demodicosis is covered in more detail in the chapter on medical problems.

The most common causes of mange in dogs are ear mites,

and these are extremely contagious. The best way to avoid ear mites is to buy pups from sources that don't have a problem with ear mite infestation. Otherwise, pups readily acquire them when for them to return to the ears.

Scabies mites and *Cheyletiella* mites are passed on by other dogs that are carrying the mites. They are "social" diseases that can be prevented by preventing

Your Collie can't tell you everything. You must recognize the signs of sickness the same as you recognize what's normal in your dog's behavior.

kept in crowded environments in which other animals might be carriers. Treatment is effective if whole body (or systemic) therapy is used, but relapses are common when medication in the ear canal is the only approach. This is because the mites tend to crawl out of the ear canal when medications are instilled. They simply feed elsewhere on the body until it is safe exposure of your dog to others that are infested. Scabies (sarcoptic mange) has the dubious honor of being the most itchy disease to which dogs are susceptible. Chigger mites are present in forested areas and dogs acquire them by roaming in these areas. All can be effectively diagnosed and treated by your veterinarian should your dog happen to become infested.

HEARTWORM

Heartworm disease is caused by the worm *Dirofilaria immitis* and is spread by mosquitoes. The female heartworms produce microfilariae (baby worms) that circulate in the bloodstream, waiting to by picked up by mosquitoes to pass the infection along. Dogs do not get heartworm by socializing with infected dogs; they only get infected by mosquitoes that carry the infective microfilariae. The adult heartworms grow in the heart and major blood vessels and eventually cause heart failure.

Fortunately, heartworm is easily prevented by safe oral medications that can be administered daily or on a once-a-month basis. The once-a-month preparations also help prevent many of the common intestinal parasites, such as hookworms, roundworms and whipworms. Please remember that Collies can be very susceptible to ill effects from ivermectin, a commonly used heartworm preventative. The dose recommended is not supposed to cause problems in Collies, but some do react even to extremely small doses. There are alternatives available so cautiously consider if you ever need to expose your Collie to ivermectin, even in small doses.

Prior to giving any preventative medication for heartworm, an antigen test (an immunologic test that detects heartworms) should be performed by a veterinarian, since it is dangerous to give the medication to dogs that harbor the parasite. Some experts also recommend a microfilarial test, just to be doubly certain. Once the test results show that the dog is free of heartworms, the preventative therapy can be commenced. The length of time the heartworm preventatives must be given depends on the length of the mosquito season. In some parts of the country, dogs are on preventative therapy year-round. Heartworm vaccines may soon be available, but the preventatives now available are easy to administer, inexpensive and quite safe.

INTESTINAL PARASITES

The most important internal parasites in dogs are roundworms, hookworms, tapeworms and whipworms. Roundworms are the most common. It has been estimated that 13 trillion roundworm eggs are discharged in dog feces every day! Studies have shown that 75% of all pups carry roundworms and start shedding them by three weeks of age. People are infected by exposure to dog feces containing infective roundworm eggs, not by handling pups. Hookworms can cause a disorder known as cutaneous larva migrans in people. In dogs, they are most dangerous to puppies since they latch onto the intestines and suck blood. They can cause anemia and even death when they are present in large numbers. The most common tapeworm is *Dipylidium caninum*, which is spread by fleas. However, another tapeworm (*Echinococcus multilocularis*) can cause fatal disease in people and can be spread to people from dogs. Whipworms live in the lower aspects of the intestines. Dogs get whipworms by consuming infective larvae. However, it may be another three months before they start shedding them in their stool, greatly complicating diagnosis. In other words, dogs can be infected by whipworms, but fecal evaluations are usually negative until the dog starts passing those eggs three months after being infected.

Other parasites, such as coccidia, *Cryptosporidium*, *Giardia* and flukes can also cause problems in dogs. The best way to prevent all internal parasite problems is to have pups dewormed according to your veterinarian's recommendations, and to have parasite checks done on a regular basis, at least annually.

If your puppy is showing signs of lethargy or restlessness, it may be time to visit the veterinarian. When your pup isn't feeling well, his behavior will likely become suddenly different.

VIRAL INFECTIONS

Dogs get viral infections such as distemper, hepatitis, parvovirus and rabies by exposure to infected animals. The key to prevention is controlled exposure to other animals and, of course, vaccination. Today's vaccines are extremely effective, and properly vaccinated dogs are at minimal risk for contracting these diseases. However, it is still important to limit exposure to other animals that might be harboring infection. When selecting a facility for boarding or grooming an animal, make sure the staff limits their clientele to animals that have documented vaccine histories. This is in everyone's best interest. Similarly, make sure your veterinarian has a quarantine area for infected dogs and that animals aren't admitted for surgery, boarding, grooming or diagnos-

Despite the effectiveness of vaccinations, viral infections can be transmitted from dog to dog, so it's wise to limit your Collie's interaction with unknown canines.

tic testing without up-to-date vaccinations. By controlling exposure and ensuring vaccination, your pet should be safe from these potentially devastating diseases.

It is beyond the scope of this book to settle all the controversies of vaccination, but they are worth mentioning. Should vaccines be combined in a single injection? It's convenient and cheaper to do it this way, but might some vaccine ingredients interfere with others? Some say yes, some say no. Are vaccine schedules designed for convenience or effectiveness? Mostly convenience. Some ingredients may only need to be given every two or more years. Research is incomplete. Should the dose of the vaccine vary with weight or should a Collie receive the same dose as a Great Dane and a Chihuahua? Good questions, no definitive answers. Finally, should we be using modified-live or inactivated vaccine products? There is no short answer for this debate. Ask your veterinarian and do a lot of reading yourself!

CANINE COUGH

Canine infectious tracheo-bronchitis, also known as canine cough and kennel cough, is a contagious viral/bacterial dis-ease that results in a hacking cough that may persist for many weeks. It is common wherever dogs are kept in close quarters, such as kennels, pet stores, grooming parlors, dog shows, training classes, and even veterinary clinics. The condition doesn't respond well to most medications, but eventually clears spontaneously over a course of many weeks. Pneumonia is a possible but uncommon complication.

Prevention is best achieved by limiting exposure and utilizing vaccination. The fewer opportunities you give your dog to contact others, the less the likelihood of getting infected. Vaccination is not foolproof because many different viruses can be involved. Parainfluenza virus is included in most vaccines and is one of the more common viruses known to initiate the condition. *Bordetella bronchiseptica* is the bacterium most often associated with tracheobronchitis, and a vaccine is now available that needs to be repeated twice yearly for dogs at risk. This vaccine is squirted into the nostrils to help stop the infection before it gets deeper into the respiratory tract. Make sure the vaccination is given several days (preferably two weeks) before exposure to ensure maximal protection.

FIRST AID

by Judy Iby, RVT

KNOWING YOUR DOG IN GOOD HEALTH

With some experience, you will learn how to give your dog a physical at home, and consequently will learn to recognize many potential problems. If you can detect a problem early, you can seek timely medical help and thereby decrease your dog's risk of developing a more serious problem.

Facing page: The picture of good health—the only way you ever want to see your Collie. Owners, Kathleen MacNeil and Deborah Breikss.

Every pet owner should be able to take his pet's temperature, pulse, respirations, and check the capillary refill time (CRT). Knowing what is normal will alert the pet owner to what is abnormal, and this can be life saving for the sick pet.

TEMPERATURE

The dog's normal temperature is 100.5 to 102.5 degrees Fahrenheit. Take the temperature rectally for at least one minute. Be sure to shake the thermometer down first, and you may find it helpful to lubricate the end. It is easy to take the temperature with the dog in a

Do you know what CRT stands for? It's important to know what your healthy Collie's gums look like so you will be able to recognize any changes that may be indicative of a problem.

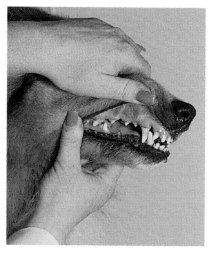

standing position. Be sure to hold on to the thermometer so that it isn't expelled or sucked in. A dog could have an elevated temperature if he is excited or if he is overheated; however, a high temperature could indicate a medical emergency. On the other hand, if the temperature is below 100 degrees, this could also indicate an emergency.

CAPILLARY REFILL TIME AND GUM COLOR

It is important to know how your dog's gums look when he is healthy, so you will be able to recognize a difference if he is not feeling well. There are a few breeds, among them the Chow Chow and its relatives, that have black gums and a black tongue. This is normal for them. In general, a healthy dog will have bright pink gums. Pale gums are an indication of shock or anemia and are an emergency. Likewise, any yellowish tint is an indication of a sick dog. To check capillary refill time (CRT) press your thumb against the dog's gum. The gum will blanch out (turn white) but should refill (return to the normal pink color) in one to two seconds. CRT is very important. If the refill time is slow and your dog is acting poorly, you should call your veterinarian immediately.

HEART RATE, PULSE, AND RESPIRATIONS

Heart rate depends on the breed of the dog and his health. Normal heart rates range from about 50 beats per minute in the larger breeds to 130 beats per minute in the smaller breeds. You can take the heart rate by pressing your fingertips on the dog's chest. Count for either 10 or 15 seconds, and then multiply by either 6 or 4 to obtain the rate per minute. A normal pulse is the same as the heart rate and is taken at the femoral artery located on the insides of both rear legs. Respirations should be observed and depending on the size and breed of the dog should be 10 to 30 per minute. Obviously, illness or excitement could account for abnormal rates.

PREPARING FOR AN EMERGENCY

It is a good idea to prepare for an emergency by making a list and keeping it by the phone. This list should include:

1. Your veterinarian's name, address, phone number, and office hours.
2. Your veterinarian's policy for after-hour care. Does he take his own emergencies or does he refer them to an emergency clinic?
3. The name, address, phone number and hours of the emergency clinic your veterinarian uses.
4. The number of the National Poison Control Center for Animals in Illinois: 1-800-548-2423. It is open 24 hours a day.

In a true emergency, time is of the essence. Some signs of an emergency may be:

1. Pale gums or an abnormal heart rate.
2. Abnormal temperature, lower than 100 degrees or over 104 degrees.
3. Shock or lethargy.
4. Spinal paralysis.

A dog hit by a car needs to be checked out and probably should have radiographs of the chest and abdomen to rule out pneumothorax or ruptured bladder.

EMERGENCY MUZZLE

An injured, frightened dog may not even recognize his owner and may be inclined to bite. If your dog should be injured, you may need to muzzle him to protect yourself before you try to handle him. It is a good idea to practice muzzling the calm, healthy dog so you understand the technique. Slip a lead over his head for control. You can tie his mouth shut with something like a two-foot-long bandage or piece of cloth. A necktie, stocking, leash or even a piece of rope will also work.

1. Make a large loop by tying a loose knot in the middle of the bandage or cloth.
2. Hold the ends up, one in each hand.
3. Slip the loop over the dog's muzzle and lower jaw, just behind his nose.
4. Quickly tighten the loop so he can't open his mouth.
5. Tie the ends under his lower jaw.
6. Make a knot there and pull the ends back on each side of his face, under the ears, to the back of his head.

If he should start to vomit, you will need to remove the muzzle immediately. Otherwise, he could aspirate vomitus into his lungs.

ANTIFREEZE POISONING

Antifreeze in the driveway is a potential killer. Because antifreeze is sweet, dogs will lap it up. The active ingredient in antifreeze is ethylene glycol, which causes irreversible kidney damage. If you witness your pet ingesting antifreeze, you should call your veterinarian immediately. He may recommend that you induce vomiting at once by using hydrogen peroxide, or he may recommend a test to con-

firm antifreeze ingestion. Treatment is aggressive and must be administered promptly if the dog is to live, but you wouldn't want to subject your dog to unnecessary treatment.

BEE STINGS

A severe reaction to a bee sting (anaphylaxis) can result in difficulty breathing, collapse and even death. A symptom of a bee sting is swelling around the muzzle and face. Bee stings are antihistamine responsive. Over-the-counter antihistamines are available. Ask your veterinarian for recommendations on safe antihistamines to use and doses to administer. You should monitor the dog's gum color and respirations and watch for a decrease in swelling. If your dog is showing signs of anaphylaxis, your veterinarian may need to give him an injection of corticosteroids. It would be wise to call your veterinarian and confirm treatment.

BLEEDING

Bleeding can occur in many forms, such as a ripped dewclaw, a toenail cut too short, a puncture wound, a severe laceration, etc. If a pressure bandage is needed, it must be released every 15-20 minutes. Be careful of elastic bandages since it is easy to apply them too tightly. Any bandage material should be clean. If no regular bandage is available, a small towel or wash cloth can be used to cover the wound and bind it with a necktie, scarf, or something similar. Styptic powder, or even a soft cake of soap, can be used to stop a bleeding toenail. A ripped dewclaw or toenail may need to be cut back by the veterinarian and possibly treated with antibiotics. Depending on their severity, lacerations and puncture wounds may also need professional treatment. Your first thought should be to clean the wound with peroxide, soap and water, or some other antiseptic cleanser. Don't use alcohol since it deters the healing of the tissue.

BLOAT

Although not generally considered a first aid situation, bloat can occur in a dog rather suddenly. Truly, it is an emergency! Gastric dilatation-volvulus or gastric torsion—the twisting of the stomach to cut off both entry and exit, causing the organ to "bloat," is a disorder primarily found in the larger, more deep-chested breeds. It is life threatening and requires immediate veterinary assistance.

BURNS

If your dog gets a chemical burn, call your veterinarian immediately. Rinse any other burns with cold water and if the burn is significant, call your veterinarian. It may be necessary to clip the hair around the burn so it will be easier to keep clean. You can cleanse the wound on a daily basis with saline and apply a topical antimicrobial oint-

Satisfaction never brought back the curious Collie. The Collie is a nosy breed and sometimes that nose gets stung!

ment, such as silver sulfadiazine 1 percent cream or gentamicin cream. Burns can be debilitating, especially to an older pet. They can cause pain and shock. It takes about three weeks for the skin to slough after the burn and there is the possibility of permanent hair loss.

CARDIOPULMONARY RESUSCITATION (CPR)

Check to see if your dog has a heart beat, pulse and spontaneous respiration. If his pupils are already dilated and fixed, the prognosis is less favorable. This is an emergency situation that requires two people to administer lifesaving techniques. One person needs to breathe for the dog while the other person tries to establish heart rhythm. Mouth to mouth resuscitation starts with two initial breaths, one to one and a half seconds in duration. After the initial breaths, breathe for the dog once after every five chest compressions. (You do not want to expand the dog's lungs while his chest is being compressed.) You inhale, cover the dog's nose with your mouth, and exhale *gently*. You should see the dog's chest expand. Sometimes, pulling the tongue forward stimulates respiration. You should be ventilating the dog 12-20 times per minute. The person managing the chest compressions should have the dog lying on his right side with one hand on either side of the dog's chest, directed over the heart between the fourth and fifth ribs (usually this is the point of the flexed elbow). The number of compressions administered depends on the size of the patient. Attempt 80-120 compressions per minute. Check for spontaneous respiration and/or heart beat. If present, monitor the patient and discontinue resuscitation. If you haven't already done so, call your veterinarian at once and make arrangements to take your pet in for professional treatment.

CHOCOLATE TOXICOSIS

Dogs like chocolate, but chocolate kills dogs. Its two basic chemicals, caffeine and theobromine, overstimulate the dog's nervous system. Ten ounces of milk chocolate can kill a 12-pound dog. Symptoms of poisoning include restlessness, vomiting, increased heart rate, seizure, and coma. Death is possible. If your dog has ingested chocolate, you can give syrup of ipecac at a dosage of one-eighth of a teaspoon per pound to induce vomiting. Two tablespoons of hydrogen peroxide is an alternative treatment.

CHOKING

You need to open the dog's mouth to see if any object is visible. Try to hold him upside down to see if the object can be dislodged. While you are working on your dog, call your veterinarian, as time may be critical.

DOG BITES

If your dog is bitten, wash the area and determine the severity of the situation. Some bites may need immediate attention, for instance, if it is bleeding profusely or if a lung is punctured. Other bites may be only superficial scrapes. Most dog bite cases need to be seen by the veterinarian, and some may require antibiotics. It is important that you learn if the offending dog has had a rabies vaccination. This is important for your dog, but also for you, in case you are the victim. Wash the wound and call your doctor for further instructions. You should check on your tetanus vaccination history. Rarely, and I mean rarely, do dogs get tetanus. If the offending dog is a stray, try to confine him for observation. He will need to be confined for ten days. A dog that has bitten a human and is not current on his rabies vaccination cannot receive a rabies vaccination for ten days. Dog bites should be reported to the Board of Health.

Collies aren't known as water dogs, and most Collies do not enjoy baths or swimming. Always supervise your Collie if he chooses to take a swim—just as with humans, accidents happen.

DROWNING

Remove any debris from the dog's mouth and swing the dog, holding him upside down. Stimulate respiration by pulling his tongue forward. Administer CPR if necessary, and call your veterinarian. Don't give up working on the dog. Be sure to wrap him in blankets if he is cold or in shock.

ELECTROCUTION

You may want to look into puppy proofing your house by installing GFCIs (Ground Fault Circuit Interrupters) on your electrical outlets. A GFCI just saved my dog's life. He had pulled an extension cord into his crate and was "teething" on it at seven years of age. The GFCI kept him from being electrocuted. Turn off the current before touching the dog. Resuscitate him by administering CPR and pulling his tongue forward to stimulate respiration. Try mouth-to-mouth breathing if the dog is not breathing. Take him to your veterinarian as soon as possible since electrocution can cause internal problems, such as lung damage, which need medical treatment.

EYES

Red eyes indicate inflammation, and any redness to the upper white part of the eye (sclera) may constitute an emergency. Squinting, cloudiness to the cornea, or loss of vision could indicate severe problems, such as glaucoma, anterior uveitis and episcleritis. Glaucoma is an emergency if you want to save the dog's eye. A prolapsed third eyelid is abnormal and is a symptom of an underlying problem. If something should get in your dog's eye, flush it out with cold water or a saline eye wash. Epiphora and allergic conjunctivitis are annoying and frequently persistent problems. Epiphora (excessive tearing) leaves the area below the eye wet and sometimes stained. The wetness may lead to a bacterial infection. There are numerous causes (allergies, infections, foreign matter, abnormally located eyelashes and adjacent facial hair that rubs against the eyeball, defects or diseases of the tear drainage system, birth defects of the eyelids, etc.) and the treatment is based on the cause. Keeping the hair around the eye cut short and sponging the eye daily will give relief. Many cases are responsive to medical treatment. Allergic conjunctivitis may be a seasonal problem if the dog has inhalant allergies (e.g., ragweed), or it may be a year-round problem. The conjunctiva becomes red and swollen and is prone to a bacterial infection associated with mucus accumulation or pus in the eye. Again keeping the hair around the eyes short will give relief. Mild corticosteroid drops or ointment will also give relief. The underlying problem should be investigated.

FISH HOOKS

An imbedded fish hook will probably need to be removed by the veterinarian. More than likely, sedation will be required along with antibiotics. Don't try to remove it yourself. The shank of the hook will need to be cut off in order to push the other end through.

FOREIGN OBJECTS

I can't tell you how many chicken bones my first dog ingested. Fortunately she had a "cast iron stomach" and never suffered the consequences. However, she was always going to the veterinarian for treatment. Not all dogs are so lucky. It is unbelievable what some dogs will take a liking to. I have assisted in surgeries in which all kinds of foreign objects were removed from the stomach and/or intestinal tract. Those objects included socks, pantyhose, stockings, clothing, diapers, sanitary products, plastic, toys, and, last but not least, rawhides. Surgery is costly and not always successful, especially if it is performed too late. If you see or suspect your dog has ingested a foreign object, contact your veterinarian immediately. He may tell you to induce vomiting or he may have you bring your dog to the clinic immediately. Don't induce vomiting without the veterinarian's permission, since the object may cause more damage on the way back up than it would if you allow it to pass through.

HEATSTROKE

Heatstroke is an emergency! The classic signs are rapid, shallow breathing; rapid heartbeat; a temperature above 104 degrees; and subsequent collapse. The dog needs to be cooled as quickly as possible and treated immediately by the veterinarian. If possible, spray him down with cool water and pack ice around his head, neck, and groin. Monitor his temperature and stop the cooling process as soon as his temperature reaches 103 degrees. Nevertheless, you will need to keep monitoring his temperature to be sure it doesn't elevate again. If the temperature continues to drop to below 100 degrees, it could be life threatening. Get professional help immediately. Prevention is more successful than treatment. Those at the greatest risk are brachycephalic (short nosed) breeds, obese dogs, and those that suffer from cardiovascular disease. Dogs are not able to cool off by sweating as people can. Their only way is through panting and radiation of heat from the skin surface. When stressed and exposed to high environmental temperature, high humidity, and poor ventilation, a dog can suffer heatstroke very quickly. Many people do not realize how quickly a car can overheat. Never leave a dog unattended in a car. It is even against the law in some states. Also, a brachycephalic, obese, or infirm dog should never be left unattended outside during inclement weather and should have his activities curtailed. Any dog left outside, by law, must be assured adequate shelter (including shade) and fresh water.

POISONS

Try to locate the source of the poison (the container which lists the ingredients) and call your veterinarian immediately. Be prepared to give the age and weight of your dog, the quantity of poison consumed and the probable time of ingestion. Your veterinarian will want you to read off the ingredients. If you can't reach him, you can call a local poison center or the National Poison Control Center for Animals in Illinois, which is open 24 hours a day. Their phone number is 1-800-548-2423. There is a charge for their service, so you may need

to have a credit card number available.

Symptoms of poisoning include muscle trembling and weakness, increased salivation, vomiting and loss of bowel control. There are numerous household toxins (over 500,000). A dog can be poisoned by toxins in the garbage. Other poisons include pesticides, pain relievers, prescription drugs, plants, chocolate, and cleansers. Since I own small dogs I don't have to worry about my dogs jumping up to the kitchen counters, but when I owned a large breed she would clean the counter, eating all the prescription medications.

Your pet can be poisoned by means other than directly ingesting the toxin. Ingesting a rodent that has ingested a rodenticide is one example. It is possible for a dog to have a reaction to the pesticides used by exterminators. If this is suspected you should contact the exterminator about the potential dangers of the pesticides used and their side effects.

Don't give human drugs to your dog unless your veterinarian has given his approval. Some human medications can be deadly to dogs.

PORCUPINE QUILLS

Removal of quills is best left up to your veterinarian since it can be quite painful. Your unhappy dog would probably appreciate being sedated for the removal of the quills.

SEIZURE (CONVULSION OR FIT)

Many breeds, including mixed breeds, are predisposed to seizures, although a seizure may be secondary to an underlying medical condition. Usually a seizure is not considered an emergency unless it lasts longer than ten minutes. Nevertheless, you should notify your veterinarian. Dogs do not swallow their tongues. Do not handle the dog's mouth since your dog probably cannot control his actions and may inadvertently bite you. The seizure can be mild; for instance, a dog can have a seizure standing up. More frequently the dog will lose consciousness and may urinate and/or defecate. The best thing you can do for your dog is to put him in a safe place or to block off the stairs or areas where he can fall.

SEVERE TRAUMA

See that the dog's head and neck are extended so if the dog is unconscious or in shock, he is able to breathe. If there is any vomitus, you should try to get the head extended down with the body elevated to prevent vomitus from being aspirated. Alert your veterinarian that you are on your way.

SHOCK

Shock is a life threatening condition and requires immediate veterinary care. It can occur after an injury or even after severe fright. Other causes of shock are hemorrhage, fluid loss, sepsis, toxins, adrenal insufficiency, cardiac failure, and anaphylaxis. The symptoms are a rapid weak pulse, shallow breathing, dilated pupils, subnormal temperature, and muscle weakness. The capillary refill time (CRT) is slow, taking longer than two seconds for normal gum color to return. Keep the dog warm while transporting him to the veterinary clinic. Time is critical for survival.

SKUNKS

Skunk spraying is not necessarily an emergency, although it would be in my house. If the dog's eyes are sprayed, you need to rinse them well with water. One remedy for deskunking the dog is to wash him in tomato juice and follow with a soap and water bath. The newest remedy is bathing the dog in a mixture of one quart of three percent hydrogen peroxide, quarter cup baking soda, and one teaspoon liquid soap. Rinse well. There are also commercial products available.

RECOMMENDED READING

DR. ACKERMAN'S DOG BOOKS FROM T.F.H.

OWNER'S GUIDE TO DOG HEALTH
TS-214, 432 pages
Over 300 color photographs
Winner of the 1995 Dog Writers Association of America's Best Health Book, this comprehensive title gives accurate, up-to-date information on all the major disorders and conditions found in dogs. Completely illustrated to help owners visualize signs of illness, different states of infection, procedures and treatment, it covers nutrition, skin disorders, disorders of the major body systems (reproductive, digestive, respiratory), eye problems, vaccines and vaccinations, dental health and more.

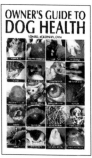

SKIN & COAT CARE FOR YOUR DOG
TS-249 224 pages
Over 200 color photographs
Dr. Ackerman, a specialist in the field of dermatology and a Diplomate of the American College of Veterinary Dermatology, joins 14 of the world's most respected dermatologists and other experts to produce an extremely helpful manual on the dog's skin. Coat and skin problems are extremely common in the dog, and owners need to better understand the conditions that affect their dog's coats. The book details everything from the basics of parasites and mange to grooming techniques, medications, hair loss and more.

DOG BEHAVIOR AND TRAINING
Veterinary Advice for Owners
TS-252, 292 pages
Over 200 color photographs
Joined by co-editors Gary Landsberg, DVM and Wayne Hunthausen, DVM, Dr. Ackerman and about 20 experts in behavioral studies and training set forth a practical guide to the common problems owners experience with their dogs. Since behavioral disorders are the number-one reason for owners to abandon a dog, it is essential for owners to understand how the dog thinks and how to correct him if he misbehaves. The book cover socialization, selection, rewards and punishment, puppy-problem prevention, excitable and disobedient behaviors, sexual behaviors, aggression, children, stress and more.